Dave Krehbiel's deep-rooted devotion to expressing m̶
has always set him apart. His memoir tells of his journey from a small town
in Central California to the biggest stages in the classical music world, com-
plete with life lessons, practical jokes, and insider views of some of the most
well-known figures in the orchestral world. A must-read for any music lover.

—**Robert Ward**, San Francisco Symphony, principal horn

Through the Door provides the next generation of horn musicians vivid
stories from the adventures of one of the most important performers and
teachers of the twentieth century. I am thrilled to have been able to join
him on some of his adventures. Reading this book brought back memo-
ries of David's musical artistry and many smiles and tears. In the stories
themselves I found important musical, horn, and life lessons and wisdom.
The Appendices A-D are important sections that I want all of my former,
current, and future students to read.

—**Gail Williams**, Chicago Symphony, former associate principal
horn, professor at Northwestern University

Dave Krehbiel relates a humorous yet moving story detailing his fantastic
musical experiences performing and teaching the horn. In many places I
had to stop reading because I laughed so hard I had tears in my eyes and
couldn't see the pages!

—**Tony (Anthony) Plog**, composer

This book is a gem. Hilarious, moving, and full of great stories and life les-
sons. A fantastic, fun read! Thank you Dave for your artistry as a musician
and a storyteller.

—**Don Greene**, PhD, peak performance psychologist

Through the Door is a wonderful book. The reader travels along through
the life of a great horn player and human being. Krehbiel is a fantastic
storyteller, and there are fun episodes on almost every page. Along the way
he also shares tricks of the trade, and thoughts on finding good balance,
in life, in teaching, and in being an honest and emotional performer in
music. What a treat!

—**Frøydis Ree Wekre**, Professor emerita,
Norwegian Academy of Music

THROUGH

the

DOOR

THROUGH

the

DOOR

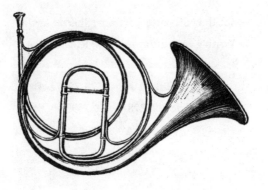

A Horn-Player's Journey

DAVID KREHBIEL

With R.A. *Krause*

Mixed-media pastel cover art: Sherri Martin
Writing and editing services: R.A. Krause

Paperback ISBN: 978-0-578-73972-4
eBook ISBN: 978-0-578-73973-1

*This book is dedicated to my wife Carol
and to all my students, teachers, and conductors
who put up with me during this wonderful career.*

*My sincerest thanks to Mark Adams, Annie Bosler, Ann
Ellsworth, Marilyn Bone Kloss, R.A. Krause, Carol Krehbiel,
Denny Mason, and Frøydis Ree Wekre, whose work and
dedication made this book happen.*

*The painting on the front cover is by artist Sherri Martin. I
bought this painting many years ago, intrigued by the image of
a person stepping through a doorway into a new dimension. I
didn't realize at the time that a book would come out of it!*

CONTENTS

I had a dream once — about meeting myself as I came through a door, and the entity I met scared the hell out of me.

In this dream, I stood waiting at the airport to meet my soul, which was due on the next plane. This was in the days before jetways, when you'd meet the passengers outside as they descended the stairs from the plane. The plane arrived and landed, and as the passengers stepped out, I eagerly scanned each one. I didn't know exactly what my soul would look like, but I knew that I would recognize it as soon as I laid eyes on it. I imagined it would be something glowing, young, smiling, and wearing a halo.

As I stood watching, lots of beautiful, happy children stepped out of the plane, but I didn't recognize any of them as my soul. Well-dressed older people started coming out the door and down the stairs, smiling and waving, but I still didn't see my soul. They kept coming, getting older and older. None of them were my soul. The last few passengers straggled out one by one, and I figured I must have gotten the wrong plane.

Finally as I turned to leave, I peered one last time through the open door and gaped in horror as an utterly terrifying form — something completely alien to me — slowly emerged. Unable to face this entity, I turned and hurried away. I knew that was my soul, and I couldn't bear to see what else might be attached to that thing beginning to descend from the plane.

◗

I've never been able to forget that dream. Why was I so terrified of my soul emerging from the door of an airplane? I've since come to understand that the fear I experienced in my dream represented, for one thing, my terror of uncovering some unknown imperfection about myself before an audience, or the injury to my ego if a performance went badly. I suffered so much anxiety before a performance that once I wished to be in a car crash on the way to a concert rather than face performing when I got there.

In my moments of greatest challenge, it has become a goal of mine to stay and face head-on, without fear, whatever is coming through any door that opens to me in my life's journey. If I were going to survive in my career as a musician, I had to learn that during a performance I must let go of the memories of what had happened in the past and my fears of what might happen in the future. I began to realize that if I immersed myself fully in the enjoyment of playing music in the present moment, I would be fine no matter what came through the door.

I came to call this attitude Creative Not Caring, and as you will see, it enabled me to face not only my soul as it came through the door of the airplane in my dream, but the many other challenges that confronted me each time I stepped through another door into a new chapter of my life.

Twenty-one years after retiring, I'm finding myself reminiscing about the doors that opened onto forty years of making a living playing French horn in the Chicago, Detroit, and San Francisco symphony orchestras. Playing horn with these magnificent orchestras was a dream come true. The ability to make a living by playing and teaching the music I loved on the instrument I loved was a gift from my ancestors and from my upbringing. Being in the right place at the right time to go through the doors that opened to me was a life-long on-the-job training because behind every door that opened was also a lesson.

Join me as I share a few of these lessons, as well as some of the adventures I had along the way that made my career such a magical journey of self-discovery and joy.

PART I

❧

THE YOUNG MUSICIAN
(1936–1957)

1. THE SHOWER HOSE

My first instrument was the shower hose! I discovered it by accident when I was in third grade. We lived in the house my grandfather built in Reedley, California in 1910. The bathroom had no shower but it did have a huge bathtub with a long hose attached to the faucet that served as our shower. I discovered the harmonic series with that hose by detaching the end of it from the faucet, placing it to my lips, and buzzing through it. I could get several different notes out of it, and I made the most of them. Welcome to the natural harmonic series and my career as a brass player!

In 1910 my grandparents, H. J. and Lydia Krehbiel, moved from Ohio to Reedley, California, so that my grandfather, a minister, could accept a position as founding pastor of the new First Mennonite Church. He built the large white two-story house on Reed Avenue that became our family home. My dad was born in that house, and my grandfather married my parents — Arthur J. Krehbiel and Corinne Gerber — in that house once they finished college in Bluffton, Ohio.

Music came naturally to me. I was surrounded by music most of the day. Noted for its music, the First Mennonite Church where I was raised had several choirs. My first memories of performing are singing in the youth choir, but, most of all, youth choir was where my lifelong resistance to authority began to show itself publicly, where my friends and I taunted our conductor, Mr. Harder, until he'd let us out early.

My father, who later became Reedley's mayor, sang in both the adult mixed choir and the men's chorus. The congregation sang hymns in four-part harmony so beautifully that it seemed you were standing in the middle of one massive choir. And my mother, an accomplished pianist and organist, accompanied them all.

Not only was the church filled with music, but our house was alive with musical activity. Every day after school, kids streamed in for piano lessons with my mother. My three younger sisters, Lora, Julie, and Donna practiced the piano when it was free, and in the evenings we would stand around the piano singing together while my mother played. At night I would fall asleep in my upstairs bedroom as I listened to my mother playing Chopin in the living room. When I hear Chopin now, I become that kid again listening to my mother play me to sleep.

My mother encouraged me to find my musical niche in the family. She wanted me to be a violinist because her older brother was a violinist; however, I caught the middle finger of my left hand in a sulfur machine when I was eight and cut the tip off. The surgeon had been able to sew it back on, but the accident thwarted any hopes of a violin career for me.

Next, my mother tried to teach me to play the piano. I took lessons for a while and could read a line of notes pretty well, but I had no aptitude for recognizing so many notes at once, or the coordination for playing them all at the same time with both hands.

My three younger sisters were all successful pianists. I believed that the reason I couldn't play was that I was just not smart enough.

I'd proved that over and over in school where I couldn't keep up with the other kids in reading, and my spelling was terrible. I couldn't remember words or recognize them on the pages. My mind would go blank, and I'd have to start from scratch with every word, sound it out and then improvise a spelling that was usually wrong. I hadn't a clue then — no one did — but later in my adult life I discovered that I'd been dyslexic all along.

Teachers did know how to make a kid feel stupid. Once during a classroom discussion about golf I dared raise my hand with a ques-

tion. I didn't understand golf, and had always been curious about what happened to the ball after it went into the hole. I imagined maybe there was a pipeline under the ground like in a pinball machine that took it where it needed to go. But I wasn't sure, so I asked. The teacher got mad. She thought I was being a smart-ass.

ʊ

2. THE TRUMPET

I've always preferred to figure things out for myself, and that included finding my musical niche. Since the shower hose was such fun, I decided in fourth grade that I would take trumpet lessons from the music teacher at school. I soon found that he didn't have nearly as much fun with music as I did. Every time I made a mistake he tapped the bell of my trumpet, which caused the mouthpiece to fly up and hit me under the nose. This was discouraging at times and not much fun, but I kept at it in spite of the teacher and quickly learned to play the trumpet quite well for a fourth grader.

Of course my family, who had been concerned about my problems in school, was happy about my new interest and my skill with the trumpet. While I was still in fourth grade, my uncle Victor, a music teacher, bought a used cornet for me. When I unlatched its case, I got my first whiff of essence-of-trumpet-in-a-case. Whew! He told me it was just the musty smell brass instruments got from being closed up for a while. I carefully took it out of the case, awed to be holding this magic thing I was going to make sounds with. I decided the smell wasn't that bad. In fact, I kind of liked it.

I began to use music to cover up my scholastic shortcomings. With the trumpet, I was able to remember the notes on the staff and how to play them. I didn't need to memorize spellings or times tables.

Since I listened only to classical music and paid no attention to what the other kids listened to, I completely missed out on the whole popular music scene. In fact, I became such a classical music "geek" that at night while everyone else slept, I tuned in to KSL, the classical music station from Salt Lake City. It was always an adventure, an awakening of a new musical emotion, when they played a piece that I'd never heard before.

By the time I reached seventh grade, I was ready for my first real trumpet solo. Until then, I had not done much performing except for singing in the youth choir at church. Every Christmas the church choir performed the *Messiah* with my mother providing accompaniment at the organ. I was thrilled to play the solo in "The Trumpet Shall Sound," even though I played it an octave lower than written. Since that first performance, the *Messiah* has been an important work for me. Recently I bought several recordings of the *Messiah* and listened to them over and over until I could select what I felt were my favorites from all the solos and choruses. Then I put my chosen selections together on a CD, creating a composite of my favorites. (By the way, I still use CD's. I'd never buy a car without a CD player!)

The music, particularly organ music, was really the only reason I liked going to church as a kid. Otherwise, church bored me, especially sermons. And I resented being told I would go to hell if I didn't believe in things that seemed impossible to me. I spent my time in church daydreaming, sometimes obsessing about why school was so hard for me when it was easy for my friends. Was I a human at all? Or was I a machine? Sometimes I thought maybe I was a machine. But one thing was certain — I never tired of the music.

After the *Messiah,* I began to have other opportunities to perform. Two eighth-grade boys and I, a seventh grader, formed a trumpet trio. We played a piece called "The Holy City" in a school assembly, and boy, did we think we were great! Our music teacher thought so, too, and arranged to have us play on a local Fresno radio station (this was 1948, and TV was still in the future).

After our radio performance, I decided I should be the bugler at YMCA camp that summer.

As it happened, the director of the camp lived across the street from us, so I knocked on his door and announced that I wanted to be the bugler for YMCA camp that summer. He hesitated, then said, "Oh, you do, huh? Well, do you think you can do it?"

"Are you kidding? Didn't you hear me play on the radio?" I asked enthusiastically. I was certain the whole world had heard our trumpet trio play "The Holy City" on the radio that summer.

It turned out the director had not heard me but was willing to give me a chance. The first evening of YMCA camp, with the campers assembled around the flagpole at Sequoia Lake waiting for the lowering of the flag, I stood proudly, trumpet ready, all eyes on me. The director called, "Sound 'Retreat!'"

I brought my trumpet to my lips. *Now what do I do?* Only then did it occur to me that I had no idea what the tune for 'Retreat' was. I looked at the director who was looking down at me with raised eyebrows.

"Well?" he said.

"I don't know what to play!" I whispered to him.

He looked a little disgusted. But, kind man that he was, he invited me into his office where he kept a book with all the bugle calls I needed to know for camp.

I learned the tunes, and the next day I successfully played "Retreat," although my inability to do so when first requested remains one of the most humiliating experiences of many in my musical career.

◡〜

---

3. THE HORN

Before I started at Reedley High School in 1950, my parents took me to a Fresno State College Orchestra concert so that I could hear a well-known trumpet teacher, Professor Schwarz. I was excited that not only was I able to get a front row seat, which in this auditorium was on the same level as the orchestra, but I was seated right next to Professor Schwarz. I would be able to see every move he made and hear every note.

But when the orchestra started to play, what captivated me instead was the man with a French horn sitting in front of the trumpet player. I fell in love with

First High School Band Uniform

the sound of that horn as soon as I heard it. It was dark and mellow, not shrill or brash like the trumpet. It matched the sound I really wanted to make. The man playing the horn that night was Dr. Jim Winter, and hearing him play marked the end of my trumpet career.

In the fall, I asked the band director at Reedley High School for a French horn to replace my trumpet, and that eighteen feet of brass tubing became the center of my life, my inspiration, and my identity. Dr. Winter became my role model.

13

Jim Winter had been a naval officer in World War II and became someone I greatly admired and respected as a horn player and person of discipline; he was in many ways my opposite, in that I was undisciplined, unsuccessful in school, and already a pacifist.

During my high school years, I drove about 60 miles round trip between Reedley and Fresno for lessons with Dr. Winter. Each year of high school l also participated in the county-wide honor orchestras, where I was soon playing principal horn and where I first performed the famous solo in Tchaikovsky's Fifth Symphony, an experience I would have many more times over the years to come. I was thrilled to be studying with Dr. Winter. I began learning the intricacies of playing the horn and manipulating the sound to get the musical effect I wanted. I knew early on that when I graduated from high school, I would want to go to Fresno State where he taught so I could continue studying with him.

Incidentally, while attending Reedley High School and commuting to Fresno to study music, I met a cute freshman flute player named Carol Smeds. Soon we were dating and driving to Fresno together for our music lessons. Sixty-five years later, we are still driving to Fresno together. Only now, to our medical appointments and Costco.

Interlochen

In 1953, the summer after my junior year in high school, I attended Interlochen, the famous national summer music camp in Michigan. This was one of the high points in my young horn career. At Interlochen, my introduction to the rich repertoire of symphonic literature began. I was thrilled by the spectacular trumpet fanfare in the middle of Smetana's *Wallenstein's Camp* (I'd always kept a soft spot for the trumpet. I just didn't want to play one). I was astounded by the drama of the Sibelius Second Symphony sweeping through contrasting vast spaces of darkness and joy. It was all new to me!

Interlochen 1953

But what had the biggest effect on me that summer at Interlochen was the music of composer Paul Hindemith, particularly the *Symphonic Metamorphosis* with its jazzy swing in the horn section that you could dance to, and its powerful ending featuring the horns. This music began my life-long reverence of Hindemith and his music. When I played Hindemith, I was in heaven.

The High D Club and Audition Mania

At Interlochen, we had a "High D Club" for young horn players who could play that note. As a horn-player, the highest note you were expected to be able to play was high C. High D is the note above that! Handel wrote a high D in a passage of his Oratorio *Judas Maccabeus*, the name of which might also be considered to have a rueful aptness by the countless horn players who have been betrayed by that notorious passage. In order to be accepted into the club, you had to play this passage a couple of times without failing. I passed the initiation and felt privileged to belong!

Altogether there were 16 horn players at Interlochen including me, and we had to audition every week for positions in the orchestra, from 1 through 16. I was always around 5th. There were some really good players in front of me. They probably went on to be doctors or something.

Dick Olberg was one of those who was always ahead of me in auditions at the camp. Ten years later, he was to become my assistant in my last year as co-principal with the Chicago Symphony Orchestra. Dick was never happy with this arrangement, and after I left he became the third horn until his retirement. I can't blame him for not being happy as my assistant.

The horn players had already auditioned and were ranked for the last week's concerts at camp, but in a kind of audition mania, the powers-that-be insisted that we hold auditions again. A substitute teacher who was also an administrator came in for this last audition of the horn section.

We decided that since he was an administrator and probably knew nothing about the horn, we could play a practical joke on him. We would rotate the section so that Number 1 would be demoted to 16 and 16 would become Number 1. Number 16 would challenge number 1 and if we voted 16 the winner they would trade places. This meant that Number 1 would have to deliberately miss notes and sound nervous, and Number 16 would have to play to the very best of his ability for us to vote for them to switch places. Likewise, Number 15 became Number 2, and Number 2 became Number 15.

About halfway through the rotation, the substitute finally caught on to what we were doing and really lost it, just furious that we would do this to him. The head of the camp, Joe Maddy himself, came in and lectured us, threatening to send us all home. We just sat and smirked at him. *Sure, send us all home and play the final concerts without any horns! How are you going to do that?* Needless to say, we stayed for the final concerts.

Those of us in Cabin 13 had a counselor that summer who was college age or a little more. Did we ever torment him! Every night "Lights Out" was supposed to mean *quiet*. But it was our cue to tell jokes and carry on. So the counselor would have to rush in and shout "Quiet!" We would be quiet for a few moments, only to start up again. Then he'd come running back. This went on most of the night. One day, I found a big rock and hoisted it up onto my bed. I had chosen an upper bunk. My idea was to push it out of the bed when the lights went out and let it thud to the floor. That night I rolled the rock off the bed, but it went right through the floorboards with a very loud crash. I got by with that one. No one squealed. When the counselor came in there was complete silence.

Seniors!

By the time I started my senior year of high school, I had a gnawing desire to graduate and get on with my career, as my career path had been set long before, since third grade and the shower hose. Then came senior dress-up day, a perfect day to ease the boredom. I went off to school that day dressed in full tails and carrying a violin case. But something was missing. Yep, my pants! I went all day without them. What more appropriate way to express myself than to play the absent-minded music professor, *sans* pants!

Senior Dress Up Day

College of the Pacific

Interlochen had been so much fun that I decided I wanted to go to another music camp the summer following my senior year. I couldn't afford to attend Interlochen again, so I chose a summer music camp at what was then called College of the Pacific (COP) in Stockton, California. There I met a couple of trumpet players, Mario Guarneri and Thomas Stevens, both of whom went on to become famous members of the Los Angeles Philharmonic Orchestra. We spent time together that summer at COP and then were fortunate enough to hook up with each other again many years later when I played for a short time in the LA Brass Quintet with Miles Anderson, Roger Bobo, and both Tom and Mario. The conductor of the orchestra at COP was Kurt Herbert Adler from the San Francisco Opera. We had a great time! That was the year Dave Brubeck's *Take Five* became popular. We played it over and over.

ᖆ

4. GRADUATING

Goodbye to the Church

When I graduated from high school in 1954 and started college at Fresno State, I left the church. I was never comfortable in a church service, and I could hardly wait until I had freedom to leave. I didn't leave the music of the church, just the church itself — Christianity in particular and religion in general. To do that, I had to give up being saved and face going to hell. Or so I had been told. I never got over my resentment at being told I would go to hell if I didn't believe in certain dogmas that to me were either untrue or were being used to control me and everyone else. But for as long as I could remember, I would much rather be scared to death than bored to death.

Jesus had important things to say, the main one being to love your neighbor, but from a very young age, I suspected that something was wrong at church in that regard. It seemed to me that religion and the church had done more harm than good in the world by persecuting anyone whose beliefs were different. This had pushed me away from my church and all religion. No one knew how I felt, not even my parents, because I always showed up to go to church until I reached college.

By the time I entered college, music was my life. I related to the world through classical music, and the horn was my way of getting at the music. I no longer tried to please my parents or friends by attending church. I did, however, start to look at other esoteric philosophies that would help me to live the life I wanted to live and to perform my music in a way that was unattached to results, and open to taking chances. I was beginning to be aware that this way of life was a possibility, and it became a life-long learning process for me.

Fresno State and Fresno Philharmonic

The first thing I learned in college was to avoid English classes like the plague! My year began with the humiliation of being placed in "bonehead" English. Not that it surprised anyone. But at the end of the semester I flunked it and had to repeat it.

Again, music rescued me from mortification. In accordance with my plans, Dr. Winter became my horn teacher. He conducted a brass choir and introduced me to the brass music repertoire. Since that time, I've either conducted a brass choir or played in one. The choice between a brass quintet and a woodwind quintet was easy. I never cared much for woodwind quintet music, although later on in Chicago I was a member of the Chicago Symphony Woodwind Quintet. But I had more fun with the fuller, noisier sound of the brass quintets and choirs.

During my freshman year, a conductor named Haig Yakjian helped found the Fresno Philharmonic and became its first music director. My teacher, Jim Winter, played principal horn in the Philharmonic. Lynn Stewart, traffic engineer for the City of Fresno, was second horn, I was third, and another older student filled in the section. Although I felt intimidated at the time, this was an excellent beginning for me as a college freshman.

When I began college, the new Fresno State campus on Cedar and Shaw was under construction, while the old Fresno State campus in the Tower District was slated to become Fresno City College. As freshmen, we had to commute between the two campuses. This could be quite hazardous for students who had to go back and forth through heavy traffic from one class to another. During the late fall and early winter, it was especially treacherous when a phenomenon in California called "tule fog" settled into the San Joaquin Valley after the first rainfall. Named after the tule grass wetlands of the Central Valley, it is one of the leading causes of weather-related traffic accidents in California.

One morning, as I drove from the new campus to my next class on the old campus, the fog was so thick I couldn't see the street signs and I could barely see the headlights coming toward me. I became disoriented. In order to avoid being late to my next class, I drove a little too fast through the fog. I felt myself go over a large bump and stopped to look. I couldn't see that I had run over anything but I was able to deduce that I had just crossed Blackstone Avenue, a six-lane thoroughfare through Fresno, and I'd been unable to see any sign of it. I took a deep breath. Somehow I had missed causing any damage to myself or to anyone else.

In the summer, I was an SOB (Standard Oil Boy) pumping gas in Yosemite National Park at the Standard Oil Station in Camp Curry. The station is no longer there, but Camp Curry is. I loved spending the summer at Yosemite and often in the evenings took my horn up to Mirror Lake, stood at the edge with my bell facing Half Dome, and played out over the lake. The sound floated across the lake, up Half Dome, and back around again. My sound filled the valley. I played in open spaces whenever I had the opportunity, just to hear the resonance of that particular place. The horn was meant for this.

Jim Winter Goes to Iowa

My teacher, Jim Winter, took a year's leave of absence during my sophomore year to finish his doctorate at the University of Iowa, and I took his place as first horn of the Fresno Philharmonic.

My first solo with the orchestra was Ravel's *Pavane* with its exquisite soaring melody. As first horn, it was my duty to play it and I was excited about it. Unfortunately, while performing it I suffered a severe case of nerves. I felt like I was trapped in a pressure cooker and couldn't get out. I made it through to the end but as the last note died away, everything went black. When I came to, I found our second horn player Lynn's hand bracing my shoulder to keep me from falling off my chair.

My life was fast becoming about conquering performance nerves. Performing seemed such an ordeal that I started celebrating after concerts to reward myself for getting through them without doing too much damage. I didn't know which was worse, though, my nerves or the celebration. Once I made myself violently ill by smoking a cigar. I believe beer may have been involved also.

Lessons with Wendell Hoss

While Jim Winter was in Iowa during my sophomore year, I had the opportunity to study with Wendell Hoss, driving 400 miles round trip to Los Angeles for lessons. My Uncle Leslie, who was a church organist in LA and friend of Mr. Hoss, recommended that I come down to meet him. Mr. Hoss was an elegant, inspiring man who lived in a beautiful house on Chevy Chase Drive in Glendale.

We played the Bach cello suites together, and I couldn't take my eyes off him as he put the horn to his lips. He was so flexible, so loose, and his technique was so effortless. His ease of playing became my goal. The more opportunities came my way, the more I knew I had to learn to play with that kind of ease in order to survive in the career I had chosen.

Let the Pranks Begin

The stress and anxiety I felt when performing meant that I had to come up with more and more creative ways of handling them, some maybe not as good as others. Practical jokes were part of the strategy I developed.

In the summer of 1956 I attended an American Symphony Orchestra League conductor workshop on the beach at Asilomar near Monterey, California. This was my first contact with Richard Lert, an old master conductor from Germany who coached younger would-be conductors at that time.

At the beach, some really nice kelp often washed up. If you cut off the small end of the strand with a knife, cut a mouthpiece in it, and then cut off the big end, you could make a resonating tube that played the harmonic series when you blew into it — in other words, a really great natural horn. If it got soggy, it wouldn't play, but if it was fresh from the ocean it would be hard and crisp and played very well.

One day, I took the kelp I'd carved into the dining hall at dinner time. The conductor was sitting with his back to me, and I snaked the kelp underneath his chair and began to play on it. Startled, he jumped up, his eyes darting around as he tried to figure out what that noise was. Why was it coming from under his chair? Why was everyone looking at him? This was one of the first of many pranks I played on conductors.

In my junior year at Fresno State (1956), I performed the Britten Serenade for Tenor, Horn, and Strings at College of the Pacific in Stockton. They didn't have a horn player who wanted to play it, so they asked Dr. Winter to play. He, in turn, recommended me to help me gain the experience, I'm sure. I was grateful for the chance. The Serenade is a wonderful piece for string orchestra, tenor, and horn.

This was the first of many times I performed it. I didn't know then that it was supposed to be difficult. The Serenade is now one of my favorites. The horn alone plays the prologue and epilogue on the notes of the natural harmonic series, with the prologue being performed onstage and the epilogue from backstage at a distance. It's one of the great works of the literature.

The text for the tenor is based on poems depicting every emotion, with powerful interactions between the tenor and horn. I was so in tune with these emotions while I played that it never occurred to me to think about what happened the last time I played a solo and fainted.

That night a singer on the program cancelled, leaving the concert without a piece for the second half. Since the Britten Serenade had already been a favorite of the audience, they asked me if I would like to play the Serenade twice that night. I said, "Sure!" So I played the Serenade in the first half and then played it again in the second half.

Transferring to Northwestern

Upon Dr. Winter's return to Fresno State at the beginning of my junior year, he encouraged me to leave Fresno and transfer to Northwestern University in Evanston so I could study with his teacher, Philip Farkas, a famous horn player and teacher. Mr. Farkas taught at Northwestern University and was the principal horn of the Chicago Symphony Orchestra.

For me, a transfer to Northwestern would mean leaving my family, the third horn chair in the Fresno Philharmonic, my teacher Dr. Winter, and the world that had nurtured me all the way from the shower hose to the virtuoso solo part in the Britten Serenade. But I filled out the application, and they accepted me as a senior.

5. CHICAGO

In the fall of 1957, I boarded a train to Chicago, a suitcase with all my belongings in one hand and my horn in the other. I found my seat, put my horn and my suitcase in the rack, and sat down. I looked out the window hoping to catch a last glimpse of my parents and my girlfriend, Carol. I found them walking next to the train as it began its crawl out of the station. They were looking up at me through the window, watching me get settled. I waved at them until I could no longer see them. Then I was alone and without family for the first time in my life.

When I stepped off the train in Chicago, I felt like a small-town country hick. I was 21, overwhelmed, and intimidated by the big city. I headed out to Northwestern University in Evanston and found a little bedroom for rent in a house not too far from school. Since money was an issue, I stopped at the Student Book Exchange and got a job selling books. Then I applied to audition for the Chicago Civic Orchestra.

Lessons with Farkas

That done, I was ready to begin my studies with Philip Farkas, the reason I had come to Chicago.

Farkas had a large three-story house with a ballroom on the third floor. In the front of the house was a round studio area where he taught and practiced. The walls of his studio were covered by autographed pictures of famous conductors congratulating him on his playing.

Mr. Farkas and I hit it off immediately. He loved a good joke and I loved to tell them. I kept him entertained. Farkas had three daughters. It crossed my mind that he might see me as the son he never had.

I was a senior and could play well, so he treated me more like a colleague than a student. We had fun together solving the phrasing and timing questions in various pieces of music. The Gallay *Unmeasured Preludes*, for example, were like musical puzzles, the phrasing and timing completely unmarked. We worked on them separately and then compared our interpretations. Sometimes I thought his solution was better than mine and sometimes I would convince him that mine worked better and was more musical.

My lessons with Farkas focused mainly on the details of musical interpretation. Yet I was struggling with slurring, ease of playing, glissandi, and consistency in my high register. When I asked him about these basic technical concepts, he always said, "Kid, you sound fine! Don't worry about it. Don't change anything."

Chicago Symphony Orchestra Concerts

Because I was a student at Northwestern, I was able to get student tickets to the Chicago Symphony Orchestra concerts. For only two dollars, I could get a seat high in the gallery of Orchestra Hall.

I was astounded when I heard the level of playing of the Chicago Symphony, and I had never seen anything like Fritz Reiner. Reiner seemed to be conducting with something much larger in mind than simply beating time. He controlled his orchestra with tiny little beats that might fit inside a postage stamp, which seemed to make the orchestra work harder and produced a sound like chamber music — one hundred players that sounded like one person.

I realized later that by making the orchestra work harder, he was giving responsibility instead of taking it. At one of the concerts I attended, the orchestra played the Schumann Third Symphony ("Rhenish"), with its long chorale in the fourth movement. The high horn and high trombone were played so beautifully, I believe I wept. I remembered my own inconsistencies in the high register and thought, *Oh, my gosh, I'll never be able to play at that level.* I was overwhelmed. I had a long way to go.

Herbert Zipper

During the fall term at Northwestern, I played in a couple of local orchestras in addition to the orchestra at Northwestern. Herbert Zipper, a famous conductor who later helped found the Colburn School in Los Angeles, happened to be in Chicago when I arrived and hired me to play in an orchestra he had formed that went out in the mornings to play for school kids.

Zipper bragged about knowing practically every orchestra piece ever written (although you'd never know it from his programming of Schubert's *Rosamunde Overture* at practically every concert). So to warm up before his concert, I would play the most obscure horn solos I could think of, and he had to ask me where they were from. This frustrated him, but it was fun for me.

Chicago Civic Orchestra

In addition to Zipper's orchestra, I played in the Chicago Civic Orchestra. A friend of mine, Carolyn Foy, played second horn beside me. My first concert with them included Beethoven's Fidelio Overture, which has a second horn solo. During the concert Carolyn suddenly turned to me and said, "Dave, I can't do it! I'm too nervous! You play the solo." I assured her that I would do it. I knew the solo and felt confident that I could play it from memory.

The solo occurs twice in the piece, and as I sailed through it in the reprise, I noticed that what I was playing wasn't fitting in with what everyone else around me was playing, and that the conductor was staring at me.

I had forgotten one thing. The second time around, the solo is slightly different — it's a couple of bars shorter than the first time. I was embarrassed at my arrogance in believing I didn't need to look at the music beforehand. However, I got my bearings and continued in the Civic Orchestra without losing my position.

Invitation to Audition

Before Christmas, Farkas asked me if I'd be going back to California for vacation. I told him that I couldn't afford to go back to California and that I was staying in Evanston to work at the bookstore.

"Good!" he said. "Would you be available for an audition?"

"What is the audition for?" I asked.

"I can't tell you now," he said.

I was mystified. What kind of audition was it that he couldn't tell me about? I told him I would be available.

A few days later, I got a call from the Chicago Symphony Orchestra saying that I was scheduled to have an audition with Dr. Fritz Reiner for an opening in the horn section. *Oh my God!* I wasn't ready for that. It had never entered my mind that the audition Farkas was referring to might be with Fritz Reiner.

PART II

❦

LEARNING CURVE
(1957-1963)

6. Knocking at Reiner's Door

In mid-December 1957, I stepped inside a tower of apartments in Chicago, rode up the elevator, and knocked on the door of Dr. Fritz Reiner, conductor of the Chicago Symphony Orchestra. I had arrived for my audition, and I was petrified. The door opened, and a short, stocky man with snapping black eyes peered up at me over half-moon glasses. It was Maestro Reiner!

He motioned me to enter. If all that I'd heard about Dr. Reiner was true, I knew that I had only one chance. If I missed one note or showed any sign of weakness, I would fail the audition. With this in mind, I went inside, sat down, and took out my horn. I said, "What would you like to hear, Dr. Reiner?"

"Play *Heldenleben*," he growled.

The opening of Strauss's tone poem *Ein Heldenleben* begins with the solo horn and cellos on a low written B-flat. I had warmed up earlier that morning in a practice room at Northwestern, but had not played a note since, and the low register was not my strength. I tried to play the low B-flat, but no sound at all came out of the horn — only air.

I thought, *Well, okay, that's it! I'm done. I failed this audition before it happened.* I figured that whatever I did now wouldn't matter. I took a deep breath, set my horn in my lap, and waited to see what Dr. Reiner would do next. I was guessing he'd tell me to go home. But he walked over to his credenza and opened a book. I was sitting close enough to see that it was the brand-new, hot-off-the-press, *The Art of French Horn Playing* by my new teacher, Philip Farkas, and that it was autographed with a personal note to Reiner.

Reiner thumbed slowly through the book and then stopped, his thumb holding the place. He looked over at me and said in his gravelly voice, "Your teacher says you must loosen the *AHM-bro-shur* [embouchure] for the low notes." This is what I called a "fagoto" (my acronym for "firm grasp of the obvious").

"Try it again," he said.

The second time, the low note sounded, and I got through *Heldenleben*. I went on to play the rest of the pieces on the audition list. I didn't think I played perfectly but because I assumed I had already failed, I was quite relaxed and even enjoyed playing the excerpts. I thought I might as well have fun, since it was over for me anyway.

Then I got up and left. I hopped on the train and returned to Evanston, back to the horn studies I'd already begun.

I learned later that Dr. Reiner had been looking for someone to replace a horn player that he didn't trust anymore. He would be going to New York to find a replacement. This was in the days before audition committees, when the all-powerful conductors could choose new players without input from any other personnel, including those who might be working alongside the new person.

Part of the replacement player's duties would be to serve as an assistant principal to my teacher, Mr. Farkas. Farkas was worried that Reiner would bring back someone with an attitude that wouldn't be helpful in that role, so he proposed that the orchestra hire me as his assistant. Reiner had apparently said, "Fine, bring him in." But Farkas, being politically astute, said, "No, Dr. Reiner, you must hear him first." I knew that was just in case I didn't work out. Then the blame wouldn't be on him.

So, that was how I, a 21-year-old dyslexic college senior from Reedley, California, had arrived at Reiner's door that cold day in the middle of December to audition for the Chicago Symphony Orchestra.

At the time, I thought I might have failed the audition because I hadn't been able to play the first note. But a week later, my phone rang. When I answered, someone said, "Congratulations! Can you come down? You are a new member of the Chicago Symphony Orchestra!"

I was elated! After missing the first note? Maybe Reiner had considered me a quick study whom he could trust to follow instructions since I was able to play the low note after he told me how. My elation lasted for about four days. Then I started to realize what I had gotten myself into, and it scared the living hell out of me. If I were going to succeed at this job, I would have to get serious about playing.

My playing was sporadic, either hot or cold. Some days I would do well and other days not so well. My chances for survival in this job were nil if I had ups and downs like this. I was going to have to even things out, to discipline myself to play consciously and consistently.

At the same time, I was pleased with myself because, by accident, I had stumbled onto a perfect auditioning attitude. After missing that first note in *Heldenleben,* I was able to play freely without caring about the outcome. Now I needed to be able to call on this attitude at will, to have it available for use whenever I needed it. How could I pick up my horn and play with the ease that would make a career with the horn possible? (See Appendix A.)

I asked Farkas how I could learn to recreate consciously what had happened accidentally in the audition. Farkas said, "Hey, kid! You're fine! You passed the audition. You're in! Just keep doing what you're doing!"

But I knew that if I were going to survive in this job, it would take more than that. In spite of his reply, I went back to the practice rooms at Northwestern and got to work, not really knowing what it was I had to work on, and scared to death that I wouldn't be able to play at the level of the Chicago Symphony Orchestra.

— 7. CREATIVE NOT CARING —

The great shaman, J. Krishnamurti, when asked his secret, told his followers that it was simply, "I don't mind what happens."

Finding a way to not mind what happens is crucial in performance. The lesson I'd learned in my audition with Reiner had an impact on me that would last my entire performing career. When the outcome no longer mattered, I was able to relax and have fun playing *Ein Heldenleben* and the rest of the pieces, focusing only on communicating the emotion I felt in the music. It was the perfect auditioning attitude. I decided to call this attitude "Creative Not Caring" and it became my mantra.

Creative Not Caring means staying in the present moment, not dwelling in past or future moments. In the present moment, you don't mind what just happened or what could happen in the future. In Creative Not Caring, you trust your body (not your mind) to play the instrument. You use your mind to power musical emotion and to define your sense of time and space in the ensemble.

For me, Creative Not Caring meant getting past worrying about the times I fainted or missed the first note during a performance, and realizing that whatever the outcome, it was okay. Just play! Focus on the emotion of the music in that moment.

I was always the daredevil who would take chances. Being willing to take chances without minding the outcome is the secret of achieving one's goals. I became aware of this when I started playing this so-called difficult instrument, the horn.

We have a choice in how we think and how we react to that thinking. But again, there was the nagging question: How do I produce the attitude of Creative Not Caring at will? How do I get to a point of trusting that my body will take over in matters of technique so that I can focus on communicating the emotion and purpose of the music? How can I pick up my horn and play with the ease that will make a career with the horn possible — like the ease of Wendell Hoss, for example? (See Appendix A)

Ease of Playing

Farkas and I had our differences. His teaching and performing were intellectual, and he felt he played better after playing to the point of fatigue. So he would warm up 45 minutes to an hour before each rehearsal and concert. He would practice his solos over and over until he felt ready, sometimes as many as eight or ten times. He once told me that he stayed up all night before a recording session in the morning because he had a good lip the night before and didn't want to lose it. I asked him how that worked out. He said, "Not very well."

Though I learned a lot sitting next to him in the orchestra as his assistant, the answer, as I saw it, was not to practice and practice on difficult passages trying to get better and better. That wasn't working well enough for me. It only reinforced old habits and inconsistent performance, not ease of playing.

It seemed to me that the ease of playing I was searching for had a lot to do with the balance between three fundamental variables that I had identified when I first picked up a horn quite a few years back: air (motivation), lips (vibration), and resonance. If my playing was off, one of the three variables was probably out of balance for what I was trying to do. If one of the fundamentals is not optimal for the register and the dynamic, the other two have to work harder to compensate. When they are balanced, the body takes over and you are free to use your mind and energy to concentrate on the emotion and purpose of the piece you are playing.

It's like riding a bicycle — you can't enjoy the bike ride if you are worried about the balance. The difficulty is that, initially at least, you can't have ease of playing while you are thinking about the physicality of playing, but you have to think about the physicality of playing in order to have ease of playing. However, as in riding a bicycle, your body eventually takes over and automatically does what it needs to do. (Appendix A).

I often imagined the three fundamentals of producing sound from the horn to be like how we produce sound from stringed instruments. It's simpler to visualize how a string plays than to visualize what's happening behind the mouthpiece of the horn. You stretch the string with the bow and it snaps back like the embouchure does when the air rubs across the lips while playing the horn. The resonant length of the string changes like the resonant volume inside the mouth changes for different pitches. Try whistling the harmonic series and notice what happens inside your mouth.

Therefore, good brass playing (playing efficiently) is only possible when the three fundamentals — air, lips, and resonance like bow, string, and string length — are ideal for the pitch and volume desired. Each of these fundamentals are quite variable, so the right balance of each for the whole range of playing is not easy.

This is where the effort comes in. When they are balanced, like riding a bicycle, you can use your mind and energy for other things, such as concentrating on the emotion and intent of the piece you are playing. (See Appendix C.)

—— 8. FIRST CSO SEASON ——

When I was hired by the Chicago Symphony Orchestra, I was the youngest player in the orchestra, and everyone called me "kid."

I received a letter from Wendell Hoss, who had been my teacher in Los Angeles, congratulating me and telling me that, coincidentally, his first job also was Assistant First Horn in the Chicago Symphony Orchestra — way back in 1919.

I also received a letter from Fred Dempster, one of my favorite teachers in the Music Department at Fresno State. He warned me of what he saw as the danger of becoming a professional musician. He thought it made a musician stoic, forgetting about the feeling and the emotion of the music. Professional musicians can become hardened, he said, so that the music no longer touches their hearts. I always regretted that I never went back and thanked him for that letter, and I've never forgotten its sentiments.

Later, when I played principal horn with the Detroit Symphony Orchestra, someone said something to me that was meant as a compliment: "You are a great horn player. You never miss any notes!" I vowed then to play in a way that listeners would hear and feel the emotion and humanness of the music, and not just the absence of missed notes. I realized then that one of the keys to my survival as a performer, and even to my enjoyment of performing, was to be connected to the emotion of the music at all times and to communicate that emotion to my audience.

In the first concert I played with the Chicago Symphony Orchestra, I filled in as an extra. My position as assistant principal horn player to Farkas wouldn't begin formally until the season started in the fall. Sitting down with the CSO and playing the rehearsals and concert that first time was a powerful experience.

Guest conductor Leopold Stokowski conducted Gliere's Symphony No. 3, the "Ilya Muromets." Even for rehearsals, he was his usual show-biz self, bigger than life, wearing a black silk shirt and lit up by pink floodlights. He didn't use a baton. All motion happened with his hands, his wrists, and his fingers.

I was particularly impressed with how Stokowski encouraged freedom in his players. One of the pieces we played had a harp cadenza. During rehearsal when the harpist finished a cadenza, Stokowski said, "No, play more! Play more!" The harpist asked, "Do you mean improvise?" Stokowski said, "Yes, more, more!" The

Reiner and Chicago Symphony String and Brass Section 1958

harpist played more and Stokowski kept on coaxing, saying "Play more!" until the harpist played a very long cadenza. Stokowski did likewise during the concert.

Another conductor I enjoyed was Sir Thomas Beecham. We all thought he was a great conductor because he always released the orchestra early from rehearsal. He'd say, "You've all played this symphony before so we don't need to rehearse it." With him, we played some concerts without any rehearsal at all, and they went fine.

Reminding me of my youth choir at church, most of the musicians in the orchestra considered the great conductors to be the ones who let you out early. I was also learning that the orchestra is like any other business in that nobody likes the boss.

Reiner's Rehearsals

Rehearsals for the Chicago Symphony Orchestra were intense and relentless. Sometimes they were better than the concerts. During rehearsal Reiner would look for any sign of weakness in the orchestra. No one dared to mess up because when Reiner heard a weakness or hesitation anywhere in the orchestra, he would stop everything and ferret out where it was coming from. When he found the offending players — and he would — he would single them out and demand that they play the part again and again in front of all one hundred players of the orchestra until he could determine whether they were capable of doing it right and, if so, could they be relied upon to do it right. The last thing any musician wants to have is an audition in front of a hundred of his or her colleagues.

Reiner tested everyone. He was capable of firing somebody right on the stage during a concert, just as he was during a rehearsal.

There was no union at that time for job protection. No one was immune, not even a principal horn or trombone player, not even Bud Herseth, the famous first trumpet player in CSO and the pillar of the brass section.

Bud Herseth was the most thrilling orchestral trumpet player I've ever heard. I spent five years sitting about five feet in front of his bell, which is probably why I have some hearing loss now. He really led the brass section. We made a recording of Wagner excerpts, and Herseth always played in such a way that we could easily fall in behind his lead. We could feel him breathing and then play with him. What a thrill!

But one day Reiner decided to test him. In Strauss's tone poem *Also Sprach Zarathustra* there is a famous trumpet call jumping up an octave, representing a shaft of sunlight or enlightened thought or revelation. It's a spectacular moment, and notoriously dangerous to play. I never heard Herseth make a mistake. In fact, I never heard him miss a note in my five years there. When we got to the famous trumpet call that day, he played it perfectly.

But Reiner stopped the rehearsal, backed up before the trumpet call on some pretense or other and started rehearsing the strings. It was just a ruse, a way to get to the trumpet call again. When we got to the trumpet call, Herseth played it even better than he did the first time. Reiner stopped a second time, went back to the same spot, and gave another instruction to the strings as a way to make Herseth have to play the trumpet call again.

I think we stopped and repeated the same sequence about four times. Each time Herseth played the call louder and better. The whole time, we could hear Herseth swearing under his breath.

Finally Reiner gave up. He knew he wasn't going to break this man, that there was no chance of a weakness there. This was where I learned that when it came to Reiner testing his players, the best defense was a strong offense.

Reiner's greatest strength was knowing how to make the Chicago Symphony play like one person so that it sounded like mass chamber music. When things got a little shaky, he would simply stop conducting, and the players would be forced to reach out with their ears and connect to each other with their senses and emotions to bring it all back together on their own. As soon as they got together and sounded like chamber music again, he would deign to resume conducting.

Even during concerts, at times he would simply quit conducting and stare at the orchestra until it played together on its own like a massive chamber ensemble. It was like magic. With this technique, he made the orchestra and each player in it responsible for the ensemble, which gave him control at a different level. He was always testing and challenging us.

There was no joking, *ever*, during a Reiner rehearsal. That was a given. One time we were rehearsing *Ein Heldenleben*, and as usual the atmosphere was tense. The three trumpet players, Herseth, Nashen, and Babcock went backstage to play the battle theme from a distance, as specified in the score. We had no closed-circuit television at that time, and the only way to communicate with the three trumpet players backstage was to have assistant conductor Walter Hendl look through a peephole in the stage door and cue them when it was time to play.

When the orchestra got to the battle scene and the trumpets

started playing, all hell broke loose. There was a ruckus backstage. The playing died out, and Reiner froze. Suddenly the door burst open from backstage, and the three trumpet players stumbled out onto the stage, holding their sides, laughing.

Met with dead silence and Reiner's evil eye, they abruptly stopped laughing, realizing the gravity of their gaffe. Without a word they turned around, marched back out, and quietly closed the door behind them. Reiner, without a word, started the battle scene again, and it was perfect as usual.

Afterward I asked Herseth what had happened. Evidently, assistant conductor Walter Hendl, who was watching through the peephole to cue them, gave the upbeat using a pencil for a baton and jammed the pencil into a low acoustical ceiling right above his head. No matter how hard he tried, he couldn't yank it out soon enough for the downbeat. The three trumpet players started laughing so hard they couldn't play, and then out onto the stage they'd stumbled.

Oftentimes in CSO we enjoyed incredible humor that was suddenly quashed by seriousness.

"Great Music from Chicago"

During the 1958-59 season, the Chicago Symphony had a television program called "Great Music from Chicago," filmed live for television from Tribune Tower. In the first of the concerts, Farkas asked me to play principal in his place. I was shocked at this since I was only an assistant. I asked, "Are you sure?" He said, "Yes, you need to do this." When I still hesitated, he told me to go ahead, he would be in the bar downstairs in Tribune Tower watching the program on television.

1958 Brass Principals — From left to right in the photo: Bud Herseth (trumpet), Clyde Wedgewood (2nd horn), Robert Lambert (trombone), Dick Lockridge (contrabassoonist), Phil Farkas (principal horn), Arnold Jacobs (tuba)

The concert opened with Weber's Overture to *Oberon*, with Arthur Fiedler conducting. *Oberon* starts off with a horn solo in the key of D. Three notes: concert D, E, F-sharp (do, re, mi). There was only one rehearsal for the TV concerts. You rehearsed and then you played the concert immediately afterward.

At the rehearsal, I played my D, E, F-sharp solo, which I interpreted as part of the dominant chord D, F-sharp, A. Fiedler broke in, "No, no, no, no! You're flat!" He thought my F-sharp, the "third" of a D major triad, was flat. I thought that Fiedler, being a string player, probably wasn't used to the concept of *just* intonation that brass players employ to prioritize purity of harmony. His idea of intonation was *tempered,* or melodic, so his third was high. Mine was *just,* so mine was lower (see Appendix D).

I played my just third again for him. He screamed nastily at me,

"No, No! You're flat! Do it again."

I did it again, a little higher. "No! No! You're still flat!"

I did it again, pushing upward on a third that was already higher than tempered — damn close to a G, I would say. Then he was happy.

We got to the broadcast, and the announcer said, "Welcome to Great Music from Chicago!" Fiedler walked out and gave me the sign to start the first three notes. I thought, *The hell with you! I'm playing this my way. I'm the one making the sound, not you!* So I played my three notes according to just intonation. D, E, and then F-sharp, the third, shaded slightly on the low side. Fiedler glared at me and gestured, jabbing his thumbs up. But I stayed with my own intonation all the way through.

I was furious. I couldn't believe Fiedler had gestured with his thumbs at me on television. After the concert I went down the stairs where Farkas had been watching television in the bar. I said, "Did you see what he was doing to me? He kept motioning me to push up the pitch on the F-sharp. *On TV!*"

Farkas said, "No, no, kid! The camera was right on you. You looked great!"

Whew!

I realized later that this experience was part of my audition for tenure in CSO. In any orchestra, there is a trial period where if the powers that be are not satisfied with your playing after the first year, they can dismiss you. It wasn't a formality during the time I was in CSO, but it is now.

Also, much later in my career, I realized that my ideas about intonation and interpretation weren't the only valid ones. Validity can only be judged by how the music touches the emotion.

Slurring and Taking A Chance

At the next concert of "Great Music from Chicago," we performed Beethoven's Second Symphony. The second movement has a little passage with a high concert E, and I'd had a little trouble with it during rehearsal. I was really worried about hitting it during the live performance. I had a choice. I could either slur up to that E my old way, as I had during rehearsal, where I had about a fifty percent chance of having the note sound. Or I could try a new way I'd figured out. And I figured I had about a fifty percent chance of it coming out that way as well.

I always encouraged my students to take chances. I took the chance here. When I came to that spot in the live performance, I chose the new way and it worked. Now I had a way to slur where the results were for me pretty certain to come out right, where my old way yielded only a 50 percent chance of coming out right. I was learning that I always had a choice even in the middle of performance. Repeating old habits reinforces them, making it impossible to progress or to change.

As for the slurring? The key here was extreme connection, like a violinist would put a finger on the string without stopping the bow.

On Tour with the CSO

In the Fall of 1958 during my first year with the Chicago Symphony Orchestra, we toured New York and Boston. I was excited to be traveling with the orchestra and thrilled that I would be playing my first concert in Carnegie Hall. It all seemed like a dream.

Carnegie was crowded. When an orchestra travels, there are

many huge trunks and cases: the instruments and their cases, the basses and their outsized cases, and the wardrobe with its trunks. Carnegie wasn't built for this. It had no backstage facilities, and our wardrobe trunks were jammed into tiny rooms that made conditions for changing really uncomfortable (later, the facilities were expanded so they could better handle orchestras).

The program at Carnegie for my first concert tour was Brahms's Symphony No. 3 and Strauss's *Ein Heldenleben,* the work with the opening horn line from my audition for Reiner. The title *Ein Heldenleben* translates as "A Hero's Life," which gives a clue as to the heroic emotion of the piece.

In our performance at Carnegie, the orchestra was magnificent, the brass especially. Philip Farkas, as principal horn, played the beautiful, reflective solo that represents the end of the hero's life. It is certainly one of the most moving moments in all our orchestral horn literature. The trumpets, trombones, and tuba artist Arnold Jacobs were incredible.

Underneath Carnegie Hall on the street level was an intriguing, old-fashioned bar from the 1900s that served German beer and sausage. We liked to hang out there after our concerts at Carnegie. The bar is gone now. After years of enjoying the bar, I was disappointed when Carnegie Hall was refurbished and the old bar became just another part of the hall.

On this particular fall tour, we traveled by train from New York to Boston. I was still intimidated by Reiner. I knew he was somewhere on the train but didn't know where. During the ride I decided to go find the dining car. I jostled my way down the aisle to the next car and through a door into a narrow corridor with compartments on one side. The lights were dim in the corridor and I stopped to get my bearings.

Down the way, a door to one of the compartments opened. Out came Reiner, hands stuffed deep in his pockets. He began walking through the hall toward me, peering straight ahead over his glasses. He didn't seem to notice me standing against the wall.

I didn't know what to do — continue walking in his direction and squeeze past? Greet him? Or just stand there pasted up against the wall, fearing equally his ignoring me or delivering some verbal assault? I stood frozen to my spot in the corridor, waiting. The moment he reached me he stopped, turned his face up to me, and drawled in the gravelly bass voice I'd come to know, "Hello, *Kraybee-el!*" Then he looked straight ahead again and passed.

Boston greeted us enthusiastically. With its light style, the Boston Symphony was very much a French orchestra. Then the Chicago Symphony came in with a contrasting full German-style Strauss and Brahms. Bostonians weren't used to this kind of power. There was something about the way we played *Ein Heldenleben* in Boston that drove the crowd wild. We exited the stage door that night to a cheering crowd!

Boston was different from New York that way. New Yorkers had to be the best and didn't get too excited about what anyone else did. They always seemed surprised that anyone from the Midwest could be as good as they were. "The sun rises and sets in Manhattan," remember that poster? But when the Chicago Symphony came to New York, it was always interesting to see their reaction. We served as a wake-up call for them.

Home Again

Every year there was a 4-H convention in Chicago, and in 1958 they hired Arthur Fiedler to conduct a Pops concert for the 4-H kids. So on a Monday, the 4-H people came in and spread bouquets of flowers across the stage to decorate for their own concert, which would be held that evening.

Reiner's rehearsals for the following week were held on Tuesday mornings. Well, you can't have flowers strewn across the stage for a Reiner rehearsal, so the 4-H flowers had to be gathered up and stashed backstage.

I came up the stairs for rehearsal just behind the orchestra's contrabassoon player, a happy, cheerful guy. He wasn't intimidated by Reiner — it's pretty hard to threaten a contrabassoon player in any case, since down that low, F and F-sharp sound about the same.

As we were walking up the stairs, there was Reiner standing in the doorway of his little cubby-hole dressing room eyeing everyone as they came onstage for the rehearsal. The contrabassoon player, cheery guy that he was, said, "Good morning, Dr. Reiner! It's nice of them to leave these flowers for us for our rehearsal."

Reiner peered up at him with no expression and drawled, "Yes, those are for your *fu-nur-al*."

George Szell

I always found it interesting to compare the styles of guest conductors with Fritz Reiner's. One time Reiner exchanged podiums with George Szell of the Cleveland Orchestra. In the Chicago Symphony we were so accustomed to Reiner's minimalistic style and his method of evoking chamber music from the orchestra by forcing us to be responsible for our own ensemble, that George Szell's more flamboyant style left us rather confused.

They both made some really great music, but Szell was a very busy conductor. He involved himself with everything. For example, during the flute cadenza in the Schumann Symphony No. 1 ("Spring"), George Szell stepped off the podium and conducted the flute player right in his face. Then he had him play it again, and again he conducted him in the same way. Szell told the flute player, "Don't worry. I won't do this tonight at the concert," but sure enough, when we got to the flute cadenza at the concert, Szell conducted the whole thing in the flute player's face.

9. ASSISTING FARKAS

With my first full season in the Chicago Symphony, 1958-1959, I began my assignment as assistant first horn to Phil Farkas, my teacher who had been instrumental in getting me the job.

I had learned a lot by studying with Farkas at Northwestern, but I learned the most from the on-the-job-training of sitting side by side with a pro like him. Unlike some principal hornists, he always wanted me to play strongly even when sitting to his left, and he often encouraged me to lead while I was assisting. He'd lean toward me and say, "You play!" Or, "You're the leader now; you take over."

Assisting Farkas 1958

I asked him why he didn't just stop and rest. He said, "No, I'll play along and just coast." He felt that he did his best playing right before he became tired and unable to play. It was my job to help him pace himself so that he would be ready for his solos when they came along.

Pacing was a good thing for me to learn. One time I got caught on the solo at the end of Bruckner's Fourth Symphony. I had been playing too enthusiastically and suddenly the music became quiet, the horn part lightly slurring up and down the octaves. Because I had been straining beforehand, I was unable to play it smoothly.

Later, when I became a principal myself, I never really used an assistant as much as Farkas used me. I wasn't that kind to my assistants. As I've said, for as long as I can remember I've wanted to do things on my own and to figure things out for myself. So I wasn't comfortable delegating someone to lead on my left unless the piece was really strenuous.

Farkas was 45 or 46 years old when his doctor told him he had to retire because his heart could no longer take the stress of playing principal under Reiner. Farkas was an intense man and a perfectionist, very hard on himself. In Chicago in the old days, the principal horn played all the horn solos, even the solos written for other players in the section, so the pressure was great.

Whenever CSO played Beethoven's Ninth Symphony, Phil's job was to play the solo written for the fourth horn. He always played it flawlessly, but one time something went wrong on the scale going up. Rumor has it he was so mortified, he punished himself by walking all the way home from Orchestra Hall to Evanston.

To him, success meant perfection. Once, after playing a Mozart Concerto, he said to me, "You know, I was really successful. I didn't miss a single note." Unmissed notes were never my measure of success. I'd rather leave an impression of emotion than perfection in a performance.

Farkas had a real zest for life and was smarter than most people. He was so good at the horn that he started playing principal in Kansas City right after graduating from high school.

Use Brain for Emotion

As I've said before, though Farkas and I made a good team, we had our differences. One of the main ones was that he thought the key to everything was to figure it out intellectually. But, as I see it, if you use up all your thinking that way, you don't have any left for producing the emotion.

Again, I'm more and more convinced of the idea that successful playing is like riding a bike. You can't think about balancing when you ride the bike. And if you think you are going to get better at riding a bike by thinking more, it's not going to happen. Thinking really has to trigger emotion, and if all your thinking is used up by focusing on the physical aspects of playing the horn, there's no way to use your thinking to trigger emotion. So you are handicapped. I don't know if Farkas ever felt that much emotion, but he certainly analyzed the music in such a way that made him very successful.

He used to say to me about the famous horn solo in Tchaikovsky's Fifth Symphony, "I've played that solo so many times in my life. I've studied it. I've lived with it since grade school, and now I've got this young conductor who just looks at it and wants to tell me how to play it!"

When I was studying with him at Northwestern, he would dissect every mark on the page, every note, every dynamic, every diminuendo and crescendo. For him, the musical interpretation came exclusively from the black and white spots on the page. But for me the notations on the page are just a starting point. You can learn a foreign language and pronounce the words perfectly, yet something will be missing if you don't understand and feel the emotion behind what's being portrayed with the words. So many people play music like that. They can recite what's on the page but they don't feel the inflections or emotion behind each note and behind each phrase.

And Farkas was successful in every way, even writing a highly-respected book about how to play the French horn. But there's really nothing in the book that would have helped me do what I wanted to do. I had to figure that out for myself without help.

After retiring from the Chicago Symphony Orchestra, Farkas got a great job teaching at Indiana University in Bloomington, making more money than he did playing in the orchestra. He had a lot of horn students, he had an airplane, he bought a big house. It was the right thing for him to do.

During his last years in CSO, Farkas was developing the Holton Farkas Model horn for the Holton Company. At the same time, he was learning to fly and was trying to get his flying hours in.

Once we flew in his plane to the Holton factory in Wisconsin to test horns together. After testing horns for a few hours, we went back to the airport and got into the plane. It wouldn't start. After much playing around with a lot of controls and gadgets he found he still had the mixture control set all the way on full lean for when we were cruising. He hadn't pushed it back in to be rich to start the engine. Perfectionist that he was, he was highly embarrassed and made me swear again and again that I would never tell anyone that he made that mistake. I think I've probably broken that promise more than once now!

Our differences aside, Phil Farkas was the person who saw to it that I began a wonderful career that was to span forty years. He pushed me and supported me to take the steps I needed to take and learn what I needed to know to become a principal horn. We were close, two sides of the same coin. He was the intellectual side and I was the emotional side. I am eternally grateful that I knew this man.

INTERLUDE

——— The Military ———

I did have a military career. In 1960, I'd already been in the Chicago Symphony for a year when it began to look as though I might get drafted to go to Vietnam. I certainly didn't want to go there, and I certainly didn't want to leave this wonderful job I'd just started. If you leave it's pretty hard to come back.

One of the things I retained from my early religious training in the Mennonite Church was the concept of pacifism. There is no doubt in my mind that war is an insane activity, and that humans are addicted to it. I am thankful that I was never required to learn how to kill someone to protect our country. Even if I were face to face with "the enemy," I would never be able to pull a trigger.

So I looked at the alternatives and decided to join the National Guard.

I found out that there was an Air Force National Guard band at O'Hare field in Chicago. To audition, I had to play a few afterbeats. That was good enough for them. The band was composed mostly of Czechs from the Cicero and Berwyn areas in Chicago, traditional old Czech neighborhoods. But the Blacks were moving into their neighborhoods and the Czechs didn't like it at all! I'd never experienced this kind of racism before I got into the band. Once there, I got to know it well.

At the next rehearsal for the Symphony, I told Farkas, "Well I probably won't be drafted. I signed up for the National Guard, and I passed the audition for the band at O'Hare Field."

Farkas was incensed. "What! A member of the Chicago Symphony Orchestra has to audition?"

I went to basic training at Lackland Air Force Base in Texas. During my stint there, which lasted about eight weeks, the San Antonio Symphony needed a horn player. Someone loaned me a horn, and I got out of basic training for a few hours.

Basic training was pretty incredible. I learned how to march, make my bed, and keep my cool while being screamed at by the sergeant.

I got to know an interesting mixture of people in our little group. Among them was a lawyer, a pathologist who had just graduated from college, and some kids who had dropped out of high school. Coming from my small world of Reedley where everyone went to church, sang in the choir, graduated from high school, and went to college, it was a different experience for me to be thrown into contact with such a wide spectrum of personalities.

In the National Guard, once you cleared basic training, you did one weekend a month and two weeks of "camp" in the summer. My claim to fame was that I never received a promotion and remained Airman Second Class for the entire six years of my National Guard career!

Later on, when my family and I moved to Detroit, I had to move my National Guard affiliation. Since the Detroit National Guard didn't have a band, they put me in a motor pool, which was fine with me. So when I wasn't playing principal horn for the Detroit Symphony Orchestra, I was a truck driver. In fact, I was washing cars in that motor pool in November of 1963 when the word came that Kennedy had been assassinated.

In the motor pool unit, we had one famous person, a young pitcher for the Detroit Tigers named Mickey Lolich. He and Denny McLain were the two wunderkind pitchers for the Tigers at that time. Mickey Lolich attended National Guard meetings with us and was at summer camp as well. During summer camp, a scandal brewed because the National Guard flew Mickey Lolich in a jet trainer from Alpena, Michigan down to Detroit Tiger Stadium so he could pitch his rotation, and then flew him back for more summer camp.

The newspapers made an issue of this. Here we were spending the taxpayers' money flying this guy in on a jet plane so he could pitch a ballgame, and then flying him back again.

Mickey was quite a guy. We'd sit in our motorpool shack in the summer and these so-called jocks would show up to taunt and belittle him. *Hey, Mickey, come out and show us what a major league pitcher can do!* Or, *Hey, Mickey, you're no better than us. Come on out and throw a few pitches!* The military is full of these kinds: sports fans, hunters, jocks.

Finally, Mickey had enough, so he walked out of the shack to throw a few pitches to this jock with a catcher's mitt. The jock was ready and he stood up against the building with his mitt. Mickey went out sixty feet or so with the ball and the crowd taunted, *Okay, show us your stuff!* We were all inside the shack looking out the window watching this happen.

Mickey wound up and threw the ball right at the jock's head. When the jock saw the fastball coming he ducked out of the way — he'd obviously had no idea of the speed at which a major-league pitcher could throw. The ball hit the wall of the shack and went right through it, into the room where we were watching. That was the last time anyone came around asking Mickey to show them what he could do.

Being in the National Guard and having contact with this portion of our population was an enlightening experience. Did they give me a bad time being a symphony musician and all? What do you think?

Getting Married

On my birthday, September 2, 1960, I married my high school sweetheart, Carol Smeds, in Reedley, California. Carol was finishing nursing training at University of California, San Francisco. Since our families both lived in Reedley, we were married in the First Mennonite Church where I grew up. A brass choir played for

Brass Choir at Wedding

the wedding — six players in all. They were friends of mine from Fresno State including my teacher, Jim Winter. It was glorious getting married to the sound of a brass choir in our old church with its wonderful acoustics.

The Episcopalian priest from Carol's church married us. There was no preacher, no "coming to Jesus" stuff. This was what I wanted.

I gave each member of that brass choir a copy of the first record

I had recorded with the Chicago Symphony Orchestra, Strauss's *Don Quixote*. I had played fifth horn and was very proud.

After our honeymoon, Carol went back to school, and I went back to work in Chicago. We didn't get to spend time together again until the following spring, when she joined me in Chicago after graduating from nursing school.

Our first child, Kristin, was born in Chicago in November, 1961. Little did we know that this little girl born to a horn player in the Chicago Symphony Orchestra would turn out to be a cowgirl and excellent horse trainer as an adult.

〰

—— 10. MORE ADVENTURES —— WITH THE CSO

After four years as assistant principal, I was promoted to co-principal of the Chicago Symphony Orchestra along with a wonderful horn player, Frank Brouk, who had been principal of the Cleveland Orchestra and later the NBC Radio Orchestra in Chicago.

This was an exciting year for me. I got to play principal horn for some of the world's greatest conductors. One of these was Igor Stravinsky.

During the summer months the Chicago Symphony Orchestra would pack up, board a train, and travel north of Chicago to play at Ravinia, an outdoor music venue and summer home to the CSO.

Igor Stravinsky came to Ravinia as guest conductor my first

summer as co-principal. I had never seen Stravinsky in person, but from his photos I expected to see a huge man about seven feet tall. To my surprise, the thin, elderly little man who came out to the podium was probably not over five feet.

Sadly, Stravinsky couldn't conduct very well, probably due to his age, but he stumbled along, and in the orchestra we did what we had to do. It was an honor to be playing principal horn with Stravinsky conducting even though it was not one of his better times.

11. ABUSE

Close to Being Fired

I came close to being fired by Reiner once. Since Reiner was a noted opera conductor, we were making a record of his favorite excerpts from Wagner's Ring Cycle. One of the pieces from *Götterdämmerung* requires four Wagner tubas. I was the principal Wagner tuba. The Wagner tubas that the Chicago Symphony owned were really junk. They were old Italian instruments, I think, and not at all like the modern ones that play very well.

On the instrument pitched in B-flat that I was playing for the recording, the second and third valve combination that was supposed to produce a concert F-sharp didn't center at all. It just bubbled. When we got to that note in the recording session, it hardly came out. It was pretty bad, and in those days there was no way to fix it after the fact.

Today in recordings you can fix practically anything. All you need is the raw material and you can do whatever you want with it. But back then they couldn't, so they had to stop everything and find a place to restart and re-record. I caused the whole recording session to grind to a halt because this one note wouldn't work. We tried it again and it still didn't work the second time.

Reiner said, "Do you want somebody else to play?"

Remembering that with Reiner the best defense is a strong offense, I said, "No! I'll do it."

Ethel Merker, the horn player sitting on my left, patted me on my knee and said, "You can do it, kid! You can do it!"

So we did it again. I'd been in this place with Reiner once before, in my audition. Here again, it was do or die. Somehow, this time the note came out. If it hadn't, that would have been the end of me for sure, because even to get a second chance was amazing. That's the closest I ever came to being fired.

It was also a severe test of my performance anxiety. The job was really messing with my head. There were times I would stop on my way home to buy a package of cigarettes with the idea of smoking all the way home to burn off some of the anxiety. The evening of the *Götterdämmerung* concert, as I drove down Outer Drive to Orchestra Hall, I found myself wishing to be in an automobile accident so I wouldn't have to go on stage and play. *How crazy is that?*

In *Ein Heldenleben* there is a sinister four-note theme (said to represent "Dok-tor *Deh*-ring," one of Strauss's most vocal critics) played by the bass tuba and the tenor tuba in parallel fifths. In yet another deadly rehearsal, Reiner kept pushing the two tuba players to play softer. The tenor tuba player couldn't get it soft enough for him (I think it's easier to play softer on a bass tuba than a tenor tuba).

Reiner was unhappy, and the next year that tenor tuba player, who was also the assistant first trombone, wasn't in the orchestra anymore. No wonder Reiner inspired performance anxiety like no other conductor.

I Dream of Reiner

During this time I had a dream about Reiner and the sinister four-note theme in *Ein Heldenleben*. In the dream, Reiner, who seemed very much like Bela Lugosi, lived in a castle surrounded by a moat with a large gate. In order to summon Reiner, you had to pull a cord and two tuba players, the tenor tuba and the bass tuba, would step out and play this sinister four-note passage.

Reiner's intensity and his tiny movements when conducting inspired another dream about him which I had several times. I dreamed that when he died they froze him in a big, clear block of ice. At the next concert the stage crew wheeled the block of ice out onto the podium on a dolly, tipped him up, and set him down. We played the entire concert with Reiner frozen in this block of ice, staring out at us over his half-moons. We played a fabulous concert, the best ever, because we did it ourselves. One hundred people, one hundred percent chamber music!

Fritz Reiner was a general who always took responsibility for making you responsible. He continually pushed and challenged the orchestra to play at the next level. When he was on the podium, you felt the power of his will. During performances you often felt that he was not being helpful, yet afterwards you knew you had done something special.

The people in the orchestra who hated him the most were the ones who formed the Reiner Society after he died. War is hell but looking back from it we realize we won the war and had a great general.

New Chums! Peebles, Lambert, and Jacobs

We got a new trombone player, Byron Peebles, a fellow Californian who was a few years older than I. He was from Los Angeles and had studied with Robert Marsteller, who played with the Los Angeles Philharmonic. Byron was a wonderful trombone player and later became principal trombone in the LA Philharmonic. A funny guy, Byron called his car a *short*. "Let's get in the short and go over for a beer," he would say. I asked him why he called his car a "short," and he said, "Well, because it would be a *long* way to the bar if you walked it."

Byron got a call from the South Bend Symphony once on his day off. Their second trombone player was sick and couldn't play. They wondered if Byron could take a train down and play the concert with them in the afternoon. Of course he said he would. I dropped him off at the train station and picked him up when he returned. When I met Byron after the performance I could see something was wrong. He was quite shaken.

Byron was a perfectionist, abnormally meticulous about his playing — about everything, really. I said, "Byron! What's wrong?"

"I can't tell you," he said. "I need to have a martini or two before I talk about it."

We went back to his place, had a martini or two, and then I asked again, "What's wrong?"

In the Brahms Second Symphony at the end of the last movement the trombones sound a blazing concert D major triad — D, F-sharp, A — that holds through while the rest of the orchestra plays the final chords. Byron was playing second and was holding his F-sharp. The principal trombone player got really tired and slipped off his note (A) and down to the next partial of the harmonic series, which was G, a whole step lower. The bass trombone player, flustered by this development, slipped *up* one partial, which put him on an F. So at the end of this Brahms 2, the trombone section was blaring an eye-wateringly dissonant cluster of notes — F, F-sharp, and G. I'd give anything for a recording of that performance!

Some of my closest friends have been trombone players. Bob Lambert, for example, was principal trombone in Chicago when I was there and was supportive of me as a young horn player.

Years later, Carol and I were driving back to California after visiting our daughter and her husband in Colorado. We decided at the last minute to take a different route and drive through Gunnison.

At lunchtime I suggested we stop at the Safeway in Gunnison and get a sandwich, and suddenly remembered someone telling me that Bob Lambert had retired to Gunnison. Bob had been supportive of me during those first years in Chicago. I thought it would be great to see him as it had been over 45 years, but I remembered that he lived in a cabin some miles from town and didn't have a phone. The only way I could contact him was by mail, and he came to town only once every two weeks or so.

Well, I got in line to check out with my sandwich, and standing right in front of me with a cart of groceries was Bob Lambert! We spent an hour together having coffee and catching up. What a serendipity that was!

Arnold Jacobs

This brings us to Arnold Jacobs, the famous tuba player and teacher who was principal tuba of the Chicago Symphony Orchestra for many years. Arnold was a student of anatomy and knew more about the physical process of playing a brass instrument than anybody. He had all sorts of medical instruments in his studio, and could measure anything. We used to kid him that we'd give him an anoscope or a rectograph for his birthday or Christmas (this was before he became famous).

Fritz Reiner was conducting in Europe and decided he really liked the sound of the F tuba, as opposed to the larger and lower C tuba generally preferred by American tuba players. He bought one and gave it to Arnold, saying he wanted him to play it.

Well, Arnold didn't want to play the F tuba at all. So he took it to brass instrument specialist Carl Geyer's shop on Wabash and had him add a whole set of valves and tubing so the instrument would play in C (this was the topic of much discussion in the Chicago Symphony brass section).

When this elaborate modification was finished, Arnold went to Geyer's to pick it up. It looked like it was made of valves. Outside the shop, the weather was icy and cold. Arnold slipped on the ice and fell on top of his new tuba, ruining the whole conglomeration of tubing. The rest of the brass section couldn't help but laugh a little.

Arnold was a little touchy about this. Years later, after a concert at Orchestra Hall, I set my horn case down by my side of the car and went around to open the car door for Carol. Then I came back to my side, got in the car, and started to back out. I heard this funny scraping noise and realized that I had left my horn by the front tire. The front tire was pushing the horn case along on the blacktop but the tire was unable to get a bite and roll up over the horn. It just kept pushing the horn along.

When I stopped, I looked over and saw Arnold standing nearby, watching me and laughing. I guessed he was having his revenge for when I laughed at him for falling on his tuba.

Bob Marsteller

Byron Peebles's teacher, Bob Marsteller, came to the renowned Midwest Band Clinic in Chicago once to play a solo on the tenor tuba. We all went to hear him. It was a great performance to which he added a little show business dazzle. At the end of his piece was a very high note. He glided flawlessly up to that note but when he got there the note didn't speak. He reached up with his hand and flicked the bell, *bing*, and the note seemed to pop out as if by magic.

Afterward we went to a reception and a number of the symphony brass players were there — Lambert (first trombone), Jacobs, Herseth, Byron, and I. Jacobs said to Marsteller, "Well, Bob, that was really a great performance, but don't you ever feel bad that you never made it to a major orchestra?"

Marsteller said, "Yeah, you're right! I do sometimes, especially at the rehearsals at the Hollywood Bowl, but, you know, after the rehearsals I just get in my car, put the top down, drive on home and jump into my pool and swim around. After swimming I feel much better." Arnold Jacobs *did* play in a major orchestra, but he lived squished into a tiny house on the south side of Chicago. No swimming pool, needless to say.

ᴖ

———————— **12. WHY I LEFT** ————————

Things had been going very well for me. Frank Brouk and I "split the book" — we each played principal on half of each concert. Towards the end of the season the manager came to us and told us that Dr. Reiner was very happy with the horns, and that Frank and I would continue as co-principals next year.

By this time I had finished my degree at Northwestern. I was visiting one day when I happened to run into the assistant dean. He asked me if I knew the new first horn player of the Chicago Symphony Orchestra because, he said, he was planning to hire him to teach at Northwestern. What a shock that was! When the dean saw the expression on my face, his own face turned red, and he immediately clammed up. "Oh, sorry," he said. "I probably shouldn't have said anything."

Since this contradicted what the manager had told Frank and me about staying on as co-principals, I began investigating. Young and idealistic as I was, I couldn't believe that my superiors would lie to me. But I found out that Reiner had indeed gone to New York and hired the first horn from the Metropolitan Opera to come to Chicago. The management had lied to us.

The moment I became aware of the lie, I decided I needed to move on. For one thing, I wanted to find out if I could actually do the job of a first horn. Being a co-principal was much easier than being a first horn. If I stayed, there wouldn't be much chance for advancement, and I really did not want to go back to being assistant principal after tasting a year as co-principal.

Once again, doors opened to me — this time, not only one, but two. In spring 1963, two principal horn jobs became available, one in the Detroit Symphony and the other in the Pittsburgh Symphony. Also, the conductors of both orchestras, Sixten Ehrling and William Steinberg, were scheduled to be in Chicago for auditions.

This was before the advent of cattle-call auditions where as many as 70 or 80 players showed up at a concert hall to vie for a job. In those days, auditions were usually held in hotel rooms and had the worst acoustical conditions imaginable with no resonance whatsoever. Rather than an audition committee, only the conductor and the personnel manager were there to make the choice.

The auditions for both Pittsburgh and Detroit were held in hotel rooms in Chicago. Since I had become relatively well-known in my position as a co-principal in CSO, both conductors invited me to audition, and after I played for them, both conductors offered me a job as principal horn in their respective orchestras.

So now I had to decide where I wanted to go, Detroit or Pittsburgh. I chose Detroit. In Pittsburgh, William Steinberg had hired a different first horn player every couple of years, so I assumed my chances of survival were better in Detroit. It turned out that this assumption was correct.

I spent nine wonderful years in Detroit, not only learning the business and realizing I could do the job as principal horn, but also taking advantage of new creative opportunities as new doors opened.

Hindemith in Milwaukee

I still had the season to finish out before I left the Chicago Symphony for Detroit. During this time, we took the train to Milwaukee for a concert, which we did about once a month during each season.

In concert halls, the orchestra would come onstage and tune as the audience took their seats before the concert began. In Milwaukee, however, the concert was held in a large theater with a curtain that was always down while we tuned, separating the audience from the orchestra. What I remember most about that theater is that when we were ready to begin the concert, the curtain rose, and a penetrating odor of perfume hit us and seemed to permeate the theater. It's strange, the things you remember about a place.

I was overjoyed that at this concert, one of my last with Chicago Symphony in 1963 before I left, I had the opportunity of playing principal horn with my idol Paul Hindemith guest-conducting. This concert, it turned out, would be the last concert Hindemith would conduct with the Chicago Symphony Orchestra as he died at the end of 1963. On the schedule for that concert were Brahms's *Academic Festival Overture*, Bruckner's Seventh Symphony, and Hindemith's own *Music for Brass and Strings*. What could be better than playing Hindemith with Hindemith conducting!

I asked Hindemith to sign a copy of his horn sonata. When

I asked him who his favorite composer was, he replied, "Besides me? Bruckner." This made me happy because, besides Hindemith, Bruckner was my favorite composer.

Brahms *Academic Festival Overture* is one of the all-time fun pieces to play, especially for horn players. This piece chugs along like a cheerful march and always has given me a great feeling of joy, even when I hear it now, 55 years later.

Hindemith's *Music for Brass and Strings* is a playful exposure of the sonorities of each orchestral group and their relationship to each other.

I also had the pleasure of playing first Wagner tuba on Bruckner's Seventh Symphony. The music of Bruckner is heaven for brass players and hell for strings since playing tremolo so much, as the strings do, is tiring. As Bruckner was an organist, his music tends to be reminiscent of being in a great cathedral filled with the sound of an organ. What is boring for the strings is ecstasy for the brass, especially for the horns and Wagner tubas.

A few words about the Wagner tuba. This is an instrument that Wagner invented, pitched the same as a horn and with the same length of tubing. Wagner tubas in the early days were made in either F or B-flat. These days they can be made into a double horn so they can be in both keys. The Wagner tuba is much more conical than a horn. A horn has lots of cylindrical tubing and the last third is the bell which flares out. In the Wagner tuba the flare starts much earlier.

The Wagner tuba has a unique sound, a little like a baritone horn. Wagner used them mostly in quartets for some of the motifs in his operas, and Bruckner used them in some of his symphonies because he admired Wagner. Perhaps fortunately, few composers other than Wagner and Bruckner wrote for them.

The instruments are notoriously difficult to play and have been a nemesis for horn players over the years. Most players don't have a lot of experience with them. If a piece comes up that requires a Wagner tuba, you have to grab one, change your whole playing style, and hope for the best. It's a little daunting. There's been a lot of development in Wagner tubas recently, so the modern ones are much easier to play than the old ones.

Enamored of Hindemith as I was, the opportunity to play principal horn for him on these pieces was exciting. Afterward, we recorded a show in Orchestra Hall for television with him conducting.

Coming back on the train from Milwaukee, I walked through the train cars looking for Hindemith. I'd had the chance to talk to him a couple of times and he'd signed his Horn Concerto for me, but I wanted to see him one more time before I left for Detroit. In one of the cars toward the middle of the train, I saw the back of his bald head.

He was sitting at a table next to his wife, eating a liverwurst sandwich. Seated across from him were the CSO manager and his wife, the same manager who had lied to me when he told me that Frank Brouk and I would be co-principals again for the next season. Seeing the manager didn't bother me much because I was happy to be going out on my own as principal horn of the Detroit Symphony Orchestra.

Hindemith recognized me as soon as I walked up. "Young man!" he greeted me and held out his hand." Would you like a bite of my sandwich?" he said graciously.

Hardly!! I was way too shy to take a bite out of my hero's sandwich! I graciously declined and thanked him.

He complimented me on my performance in Bruckner's Seventh Symphony and the other pieces I played with him, and he asked, "What are your plans, my boy?" I proudly told him that I was leaving the orchestra in the fall to be the new principal horn of the Detroit Symphony Orchestra.

Furious, he glared at the manager and bellowed in his German accent, "You idiot! You're stupid! What were you thinking? You should never have let this man leave this orchestra!" My hero was attacking the manager! I stood by in disbelief watching as he continued his tirade. How could anyone dream up a better revenge scenario?

Shortly after that, Hindemith died and it was the end of an era. One of his pieces is called *The Harmony of the World.* I've got an old Berlin Philharmonic recording of it. Wow! The horn parts are incredibly treacherous in the way they jump around. There's a huge danger of playing wrong notes or what we in the industry call "clams."

I couldn't imagine having to play it at that time. Even in the Berlin recording, the players were having trouble.

However, years later in San Francisco we did play that piece with Blomstedt, and it was so much fun! Our horn section just ate it up. The abilities of younger players keeps increasing and the standards are much higher than thirty or forty years ago.

Autographed from Hindemith to Arthur Krehbiel

PART III

⌯

SYMPHONIC METAMORPHOSIS
(1963-1972)

13. Unions and Symphony Orchestras

Up through Reiner's time in Chicago, conditions in the orchestra were poor, as were relations between the orchestra players and management. The first chair (principal) players such as Philip Farkas were ranked much higher than the tutti players and were paid twice or sometimes three times as much as the section players.

Of course, the conductors were on a pedestal way above everyone else, but the tutti players were treated as mere grunt workers. Solos that came up in the manuscript for the other horn section members (i.e., second horn, third horn, and fourth horn, etc.) were all penciled into the first horn part. Only the principal players were permitted to play them.

In those days, the unions represented a kind of sweetheart deal between the management, the union, and the principal players. It always seemed to me that whenever the tutti players pushed for better working conditions, the management would give the principal players more money and tell them to keep the troops quiet. So the disparity between principal and section players became even greater.

When I started in 1958, players were beginning to demand that their union support all of them, not just the principal players and management. That's when we started demanding a yearly schedule rather than a week-by-week schedule, for example.

We demanded the formation of an orchestra committee consisting mainly of tutti players which would be consulted and have some say in the union and orchestra activities. We also demanded that a committee be appointed to hear auditions, taking away the conductor and personnel manager's exclusive control over choosing new players.

Many of us from the Chicago Symphony organized and went down to the union to demand change. We started a union magazine for orchestra musicians called *Senza Sordino* (without mute) that discussed the conditions in the major orchestras, and it's still going strong now.

By the time I got to Detroit, the working conditions weren't quite as bad. There was a lot more cooperation. Detroit and most of the other orchestras were starting to have committees, representation, and some say in auditioning new players. Also, they had more defense against arbitrary dismissal, which wasn't the case at all in Chicago.

〜

—14. AT HOME IN DETROIT—

In the fall of 1963, Carol, Kristin, and I moved to Detroit. We found a little house to rent by City Airport. It was good to get out of an apartment. We were very happy there. We even had a garage and a little park down the street.

On February 2, 1965, I was at Interlochen with the Detroit Symphony Orchestra when I got an exciting phone call: *You've got a son, you've got a son!* Friends had taken Carol to the hospital, and our little boy, Art, was born. I was away on tour with the orchestra again. I had missed the births of both our children.

But our family had happy times in Detroit. The orchestra was full of young players our age who, like us, had young children. We camped together, picnicked together, and partied together.

〜

—15. PLAYING DETROIT—

Going from the Chicago Symphony to the Detroit Symphony was a culture shock. Gone was the austere, intimidating climate of rehearsals. In Detroit, people talked, told jokes, and had fun in rehearsals. The French conductor Paul Paray — Detroit's conductor before Sixten Ehrling, who hired me — had instilled a lighter French sensibility into the orchestra compared to the more serious

Bruckner/Wagner character of Chicago.

The players in the Detroit Symphony were younger overall than in the Chicago Symphony, and the playing level wasn't as high. At the first concerts I played with them, which were children's concerts at 8:30 in the morning, just half the orchestra's personnel were present. I was a bit taken aback.

Henry Lewis, who would over the years become a very good friend of mine, conducted these concerts. Henry began his career as a teenage virtuoso bass player with Los Angeles Philharmonic when Alfred Wallenstein was the conductor.

Wallenstein was another tyrant like Reiner. The story goes that at the first rehearsal of a symphony one week, Wallenstein started and stopped the orchestra at the beginning of a piece several times, then told the librarian to go downstairs and bring up another piece, saying simply, "They can't play this piece."

One of the pieces Henry liked to play for the children's concerts was Nocturne from *Midsummer Night's Dream*. He conducted it so slowly that I could barely make it through. I really struggled with my endurance. It was a challenging, yet enlightening, time for me because I had to come up with new ideas.

As I learned more about ease of playing and the balance of air, vibration, and resonance (Appendix C), my endurance improved. I also learned that my trick of connecting the slurs, like the violinist who places a finger on the string while the bow is still moving, would help my endurance as well.

A favorite story in the Detroit Symphony was about their former conductor, Paul Paray, a sweet, happy-looking guy a little like

DSO Horn Section
Back (left to right): Willard Darling, Ed Sauve, Keith Vernon
Front (left to right): Charlie Weaver, David Krehbiel, Tom Bacon

Fred Mertz in "I Love Lucy." Once while Paray was conducting a rehearsal, a fly kept buzzing around his shiny head, landing here and there and then buzzing off again, only to return to another spot while Paray swatted and slapped ineffectually. Finally Paray became exasperated, stopped the rehearsal, and said in his French accent, "I can't understand *theese!* I take the shower every day." Somebody in the back of the orchestra said, "You can't fool the flies!"

When I got there, I noticed the horn section had a tradition of interjecting a particular little flourish at certain times — *dat da-dah* (the fifth and fourth notes of a scale slurring down to a minor third.) I learned that the figure originated as a horn theme from Brahms's Second Symphony, but what it meant to DSO was *Up your ass!* So if they had a conductor they didn't like, they would add that flourish — dat da-dah — where appropriate (or sometimes not). During Paray's time in Detroit, someone had told him that *dat da-dah* was a little fanfare in honor of him.

After I started with Detroit, Paray came back as a guest conductor. Whenever he walked onstage the horn section would play *dat da-dah*, and he'd always smile and wave at us. Eventually someone told him that it really meant *Up your ass!* He wasn't too happy about that.

We didn't dislike Paray particularly, but he was a conductor. It was universal, you can't *like* the conductor!

Sixten Ehrling

In 1963, the conductor of the Detroit Symphony was Sixten Ehrling, who was a very smart man. He could easily conduct Stravinsky's *Rite of Spring* without a score and not make a mistake. He was a cold Swedish man with an incredible mind but not much emotion; all that he required was a performance be technically perfect.

I asked him one time if he kept a calendar or notebook for appointments or notes. He said, "No, I don't need to." Of course he didn't. He was so smart he could carry it all in his head, including every black dot on the music manuscript. But I never felt he had a love of the music he conducted.

Phrasing for him seemed an intellectual exercise, never emotional. He was very confident in his skills, but they didn't work for me or for others in the orchestra. Most of us felt as though the orchestra was just a music-producing factory lacking humanness in its product. We'd play piece after piece accurately but never with much expression. I think this was partly what caused us to form a rock group later on.

When Ehrling auditioned me, it was just him and the personnel manager in the room. That's how it was in those days, a pretty cold affair. You'd go in, play your notes, and then leave. No one provided comments or feedback. You'd just wait to hear the results.

Eugene Jochum

Not long after I began with the Detroit Symphony, we had a great guest conductor named Eugen Jochum, who at that time was the conductor of the Concertgebouw Orchestra in Amsterdam. On one of the programs, he instructed me on how to play the famous solo in Strauss's *Till Eulenspiegel's Merry Pranks* in front of all one hundred members of the DSO.

That's the last thing any horn player wants. Ideally, you want to play your solo so convincingly that even if it is not how the conductor envisions it, he will leave you alone. However, when I played the solo opening call for *Till Eulenspiegel* at rehearsal Jochum stopped the orchestra, and at the expense of a little of my pride, he taught me an interpretation that really made sense to me. Since then, I've taught it that way myself.

As the piece begins, Strauss seems to be looking for a place to start a simple horn call that he probably heard his horn player father play many times. In 6/8 time, he tries starting the call on the second beat of the measure, but it doesn't quite fit. So he tries again on the third beat, but once again, it doesn't fit. Then, finally, he starts it one more time, this time on the fourth beat, and it fits. The strong notes are now on the strong beats and it works. Maestro Jochum wanted me to make this progression perfectly clear in how I played it. The last two low notes of the phrase, seemingly tacked on unnecessarily, could be the punch-line of the merry prank!

So I had the dubious privilege of playing this over a few times in front of everyone until Jochum was satisfied. He seemed to really like me after that, and he invited me to come to Amsterdam to play in the Concertgebouw Orchestra. I never took him up on that offer.

Arthur Fiedler

My disagreement with Arthur Fiedler in Chicago over the pitch in Weber's *Oberon* was only the beginning of an enduring love/hate relationship. The first time he came to Detroit to conduct a pops concert after my arrival there, he walked onstage for rehearsal and immediately spotted me sitting in my new position in the horn section.

He stared at me, looking a little confused as if wondering whether I was in the wrong orchestra — or was he? Maybe he was thinking, *Oh, no, I'm going to have to contend with him again!* After a few moments he bellowed across the orchestra, "What are you doing here!" Fiedler and I went on to enjoy nine years of repartee in Detroit.

Some of the most fun times in Detroit were playing the pops series at the Lightguard Armory, a big, open space with tables and plenty of eating and drinking while the music played. It was a pops concert in the truest sense.

The percussion section in Detroit could never seem to please Fiedler, and he was always rude about it. His harsh voice grated, and he interrupted the music often with, "No, no! That's not right!"

Fiedler was usually pretty loaded when he conducted. He always did a concert in three parts. For the middle third of the concert he'd hire a new soloist he could get cheaply to play a standard concerto such as Mendelssohn or Tchaikovsky. All the principal players would take the middle third off and let the assistants or associates play the concerto. During this break my friends and I would go back to Fiedler's dressing room and drink from his giant bottle of booze.

He finally got wise to this and began marking the level on the bottle before he left the room. So we would drink our fill and then re-fill the bottle with water to the level Fiedler had marked.

In his concert series, Fiedler always programmed a piece called the *Armed Forces Medley*. It had tunes from the Navy, Army, and Air Force such as "Off We Go into the Wild Blue Yonder." I decided I would make paper airplanes to throw the next time we played this. You could never have gotten away with this in Chicago, but things were pretty loose in Detroit.

When we got to the *Armed Forces Medley* in the concert, I threw the paper airplanes up from in the orchestra. Well, that went over big with my friends, so the next year, they all made paper airplanes, too. At the concert, huge white clouds of paper airplanes flew up from the orchestra as we played the Air Force Song. Hardly anyone was playing their instruments. Everyone was flying paper airplanes.

The next year when Fiedler came back, it was the same routine — *Armed Forces Medley* was on the program. That year I decided to top everything. I had become the horn teacher and brass choir conductor at Wayne State. To advertise the brass choir concert, we'd made posters, sized about 18 inches by 24 inches. They were made of a foil-backed paper, just the right weight and texture to make a giant paper airplane. So I made a very pointy-nosed airplane, about two feet long when folded. I fine-tuned it so that it would go perfectly straight, and I practiced flying it until it would go exactly where I aimed it.

That night at the concert, the orchestra members all had paper airplanes waiting under their chairs. When we got to the *Armed Forces Medley,* up soared the massive white cloud. I waited until everyone else's paper airplane had come back down. Then I stood up and aimed my giant paper airplane right at Fiedler.

My plane flew just past his head, about a foot and a half away. Of course, he was a little drunk at the time. He dropped his jaw and gaped as it soared by his face and disappeared out into the audience somewhere. Well, never again did the *Armed Forces Medley* show up on the program.

During this time there were a lot of bomb scare stories in the news. I had just gotten a new electric metronome, and I decided to stash it in Fiedler's dressing room, ticking away. When he returned home he sent me a letter thanking me for the metronome. He said he had many metronomes but not a new one like this. I sent a letter back saying the least he could do would be to send me an autographed picture, which he did. The next time he came to Detroit he invited me to play a Mozart concerto with him.

Fiedler was said to be the richest conductor in the world. He had more records and more money from conducting than any other conductor.

♆

—— 16. HORN WORKSHOPS ——

In 1970, the International Horn Society hosted its Second International Workshop in Tallahassee, Florida. Dale Clevenger, principal horn of Chicago Symphony, and I were two of the featured artists, and we shared a recital. Many of the well-known players of that era were present including my teachers Jim Winter, Wendell Hoss, and Philip Farkas.

I asked Dale if he would like to end our recital with a duet. "What did you have in mind?" he asked.

"Let's improvise a duet," I said.

"I've never done anything like that," he said.

"Neither have I," I said.

"Well, what will we do?"

"You just start," I said, "and I will follow you in. We can end it by you playing the opening of *Till Eulenspiegel* and I will play it with you, but upside-down."

This would mean that I would end on a high written C and Dale would end on a C three octaves lower. He asked if we could rehearse it. I told him that would ruin the spontaneity.

Before the duet, I gave a little talk about how we had commissioned a friend to compose this piece, but it had been at the last minute, and since Dale was in Chicago and I was in Detroit, we hadn't had much time to rehearse it. However, we would do the best we could. Then I set up four music stands in a row and unfolded a long sheet of manuscript paper.

Off we went with Dale glissing and trilling all over the horn and me following and mimicking him. This went on for several minutes until I suddenly stopped and said, "Dale, I think we are a bar off!" He agreed and we started again. After another minute or so we paused, then we played our *Till Eulenspiegel* ending. It was a huge hit. They loved us!

Farkas rushed up onto the stage and said he had to have a copy of that duet. I said, "You are welcome to the original!" He walked over to the manuscript, took a look at it, then looked up, shocked. The manuscript pages were blank. He said, "I could never play that without the music."

I thought, *I would never have the patience to learn something like that if I had to read the music.* However, I am sure that Farkas could and would.

Also at that recital we finished with an Anton Reicha trio with Dale, myself, and Michael Hoeltzel. We played it, and then we sang it for an encore.

Some years later and after being featured in several of these workshops, I was made an Honorary Member of the International Horn Society — a great honor for me.

———— **17. MY FATHER** ————

One afternoon I received a phone call from California letting me know that my father had passed away suddenly from a heart attack. He was 53. He had always been very supportive of my career choice. He wrote a letter to me about once a week during my time in Chicago and Detroit.

His death was a real shock for everyone, including the people of the town of Reedley where he had been mayor. Carol and I decided that I should fly to California alone since she was pregnant with our son, and Kristin was only three years old. I distinctly remember the loneliness and grief I felt sitting on that airplane flying back to California. I've always felt bad that we didn't take the whole family.

———— **18. MOTOWN** ————

In the 1960's, a few of us horn players and a few string players from the Detroit Symphony made a little extra money by hiring ourselves out as "sweeteners" for Motown recordings. Motown's original studio, called Hitsville, was in downtown Detroit in a funny old house that had been converted into a studio. We supplied backup for artists such as the Supremes, Aretha Franklin, and many others. It was always an incredible experience to go down to Motown and play with these people.

Making records in the classical world was an intense affair. Playing at Motown was exactly the opposite. You'd get hired for a session that started at two p.m., for example, and at 2:30 or 2:45 the musicians and staff would still be milling about, chatting and snacking while they waited for the arranger to show up with the charts and the music and start putting things together. Money seemed to be no object. Usually in a classical recording session you start right on time because you are getting paid by the minute. Well, in Motown you were paid by the minute, too, but they didn't seem to mind delays as much.

There were some really great people at Motown. One was Marvin Gaye. I went to meet him at the big studio one day carrying my horn, but the place looked empty except for one man who seemed to be working there in some capacity. He said that Marvin was expecting me and wanted me to play a little *obbligato*. So I followed him into a big room where Marvin Gaye sat at a piano picking out a tune.

He looked up at me and said, "I was thinking about having a horn melody here." I asked him what he had in mind. He played a little subject on the piano and asked if I could do that. "Sure," I said, and I played on the horn what he had played on the piano. He thought it sounded good and wanted to record it to see what it sounded like.

The control room was on the second floor of the studio. It was a large room with big windows and lots of light and it was full of guys sitting around eating. I recorded the melody with Marvin, and he said to the guys at the console, "Okay, play that back to me." They played back what we had just done, and Marvin said, "Okay, now all of you guys come downstairs with us." He certainly seemed to have a lot of power here.

So four or five of the engineers came trooping down with us into the big room, Marvin sat at the piano, and I stood next to him.

Marvin said to me, "Okay, play that again."

I played it again, and Marvin said, "Okay, now, you guys go up there and make sure what comes out of those speakers sounds exactly like what you just heard here." A horn player's dream! Without a word, these guys started moving in sync like they were dancing, taking down and putting up different microphones, until all was ready, and we recorded it again.

This was so different from what we normally experienced in the orchestra. Oftentimes in recording important horn passages, we'd go to hear the playbacks, and the horns weren't coming through. Even though we were playing very loudly trying to be heard on the recording, we weren't being picked up by the microphones.

Once I said to an engineer, "Listen, you've got to do something here! You don't have any mikes in back of us! You know, with the horn the sound comes out the back, not the front. We don't need a microphone in front of us; we need one in back of us."

The guy gave me a dirty look and said, "Okay, okay!"

I went back onstage and sure enough he showed up with another mike and put it behind us. "Okay," he said, "Here's your mike!" Then he grabbed the cable for the mike, and instead of plugging it into anything he threw it underneath the riser. My thought was, *You really don't want our input, do you?*

At this point I was beginning to realize that for modern recordings, the role of the orchestra was just to provide raw material for what would later be fashioned into a finished product by others.

I was very angry at this. We had no control over what was being recorded. Anything we played could be changed or fixed later according to the whims of the powers that be, so no one really cared about what was being recorded at the sessions.

This was a whole new approach from when I started, and we would have to re-record large sections if something wasn't right so they could splice the tape in the appropriate places, sometimes whole movements. It really tempted me to try to get a clam onto a recording. If I succeeded, it would be their fault, not mine. If they didn't catch it, to heck with them. So nothing mattered.

On the bright side, however, being just the raw material did give us the freedom of not having to care as much. Another application for my philosophy of Creative Not Caring, with a little negative reinforcement from the recording engineers!

〜

──────── 19. NEW HOME ────────

Carol and I were very happy in Detroit. We had a lot of good friends in the orchestra, and at that time I was planning to spend the rest of my career in Detroit.

After living in our rental house by the city airport for a while, we decided we could afford to buy a home and found a wonderful old house in Royal Oak for $26,000 — certainly not today's prices. The house had been built around an old tree which was now growing out of it.

Some years later, we also bought a little cottage near Ann Arbor in Brighton, Michigan on Little Crooked Lake. It was rather run-down but we figured we could fix it up. This involved replacing the septic system, finishing the cabinets, and building a dock.

Our cottage on the lake became a place where we could hang out with our friends when we had a day or two off. One of the trombone players in DSO, Dennis Smith, had a large boat with a big motor that he parked there at our dock on the lake.

20. PRANKS

A camaraderie often developed between orchestra members that broke the relentless tension of constant rehearsals, concerts, and anxiety about performances. It often manifested in a one-up-manship of prank-playing. In Chicago, Reiner would never have permitted it, of course, but it became apparent in the more relaxed culture of Detroit, as seen with the horn flourishes for Paray and the paper airplanes with Fiedler's *Armed Forces Medley*.

One of the best pranks I've heard about was perpetrated by Don Green, the former first trumpet of the Detroit Symphony (not Dr. Don Greene, author of *Winning on Stage*). Don had moved from Detroit back to Los Angeles to play principal trumpet with the Los Angeles Philharmonic, and at this time, both DSO and the LA Phil were in New York City on tour.

Don found out when DSO was scheduled to arrive at their

hotel. He disguised himself as a homeless person wearing a shabby overcoat and a rumpled hat pulled down over his eyes. Trumpet in hand, he sat cross-legged behind his open trumpet case in front of the hotel, and as the DSO members got off their bus from the airport, he began playing the "Michigan Fight Song," very badly.

He shocked the orchestra members by calling out their names as they walked by, and if they didn't put money in his trumpet case he chastised them with insults like, "You always were a cheapskate!"

‿

—— 21. STARTING NOTES ——

The Detroit Symphony Orchestra's summer home was outdoors at the Meadow Brook Amphitheatre. One of my favorite guest conductors there was Robert Shaw. His repertoire always involved a chorus. He was an emotional guy, very intense. When he conducted, he would sweat profusely, especially when we did an intensely emotional piece like the Britten *War Requiem*.

Shaw always wore a towel around his neck in rehearsals. So I got the idea that we should all have towels. I bought a bunch of towels at the thrift store and encouraged people to bring their own as well. When Shaw came out for rehearsal, the whole orchestra was sitting in their chairs with towels around their necks. He grimaced slightly and without a word started conducting, leaving us to sweat with our towels around our necks while we played.

I was happy to have the opportunity again to play one of my favorite pieces, the Britten Serenade for Tenor, Horn and Strings, in one of the concerts at Meadow Brook. I hadn't played it since college when I played it twice in one concert at College of the Pacific. At Meadow Brook, Jan Pearce sang the tenor solo, but it wasn't really his forte. The Serenade requires a light, lyric tenor, and Jan was a strong operatic tenor.

Massive thunderheads threatened above as we prepared to begin the Serenade onstage. Sixten Ehrling stepped onto the podium. Jan Pearce stood on his left and I on his right, waiting for the cue. The Serenade opens with a haunting solo horn call. Starting the first note of that call was scary for me. If I hesitated, it could be deadly. I could easily miss the first note. Ehrling looked over at me, indicating that I was to start. I took my breath.

Just as I was ready to let that first note sound, a tremendous flash of lightning struck about a quarter mile away accompanied by a resounding thunder clap, and the heavens opened. The concert came to a halt as concert-goers poured down the amphitheatre's grassy slope seeking shelter underneath the shed. Beer bottles and cans cascaded down the stairs in the wind. The audience stood crammed together under the shelter for 30 minutes until things calmed down and everyone could take their places and we could try again.

By this time of my life, I had become quite agnostic with a habit of bad-mouthing God, but it did enter my mind during the incident that possibly God was trying to give me a message of some sort. The whole thing sure did scare the heck out of everybody.

Having to start alone on the first note of any orchestral work is a popular subject for all kinds of superstitious tales!

As an example, Mahler's Fifth Symphony begins with a dark threatening trumpet solo. Many tales have been told over the years about the predicaments of various players starting this solo. One of these stories is set in Vienna at the renowned Musikverein. Some people believe that the ghost of Mahler haunts this great music hall. The inside of the hall is surrounded by tall granite columns topped with statuary. As the trumpet player prepared to begin the famous solo, the hall began to shake violently. Everyone in the hall had to run for cover until the earthquake was over.

Aside from superstition, it is an awesome responsibility to begin an orchestral work alone. That first note sets the emotional mood for the whole piece. It can either make or break the performance.

The closest I came to a real meltdown over the issue of starting notes involved the opening of Bruckner's Fourth Symphony. The strings begin the piece with a shimmering tremolo like leaves fluttering in a forest. After a few bars, the horn enters with a distant and plaintive call that forms the basis for the whole symphony. Making that soft entrance can be frightening. One time when we were playing a concert on tour in Frankfurt, Germany, I panicked. My body went rogue and I was completely soaked in sweat.

Over the years, I've received some suggestions that have helped me with starting orchestral pieces alone. One is to feel that the underlying rhythmic pulse has already begun. It's easier to start if there is already a rhythm going. If the timing is arbitrary, it's harder. Another suggestion I received from a friend of mine was to concentrate on the aperture at the other end of your body instead of what you're going to do with your mouth. Strangely, I find this works!

Wagner's famous horn call from *Siegfried* is another solo that can be troublesome to start. One strategy I developed was to go for the first note in a way that gives a lilt to the following notes. Then stay in character!

My colleague Ed, the third horn in Detroit, was certainly in character one evening when we were on tour in New York City. After some post-concert refreshment in a bar near Carnegie Hall, Ed took out his horn and launched into the Siegfried horn call. The reverberation between the tall buildings on either side of the street was exciting.

Soon a cop car rolled up and I thought, *Oh, no, we have a problem now!*

The window of the car rolled down. The cop listened for a minute and said, "Sounds good!" Then he drove off.

22. Symphonic Metamorphosis

Though I was happy socially in Detroit, playing in the orchestra was a musically frustrating experience a lot of the time. Our conductor, Sixten Ehrling, approached music intellectually with almost no emotion, and seemed unable to make a phrase. My friends and I felt like the orchestra was just a music factory. We were not making music from the heart.

From childhood, I'd been instinctively aware of how important it was to be in touch with the composer's emotional intent of a piece when performing and to be able to communicate that emotion to an audience. After I passed my audition with Reiner in 1958 and began playing with the Chicago Symphony Orchestra, I wrote down several characteristics I felt a performer needed to be aware of in order to communicate musically:

- Balancing the vertical with the horizontal. Feeling the flavor of each note while being conscious of the line or phrase.

- Feeling the gravitational pull from one note to the other going or coming.

- Creating tension and releasing tension in a musical phrase like breathing in and out.

- Using tone color, volume, and inflection as an actor would do to portray emotion.

- Becoming involved with the emotion of the music, which is the best way to alleviate stage fright.

- Being aware of and feeling the architecture of each phrase and composition. (Appendix A)

Out of frustration with the orchestra, and inspired by our Motown experiences, some friends of mine and I decided we would create a rock group from members of the Detroit Symphony. Erv Monroe (the principal flute player), Bob Cowart, and I came up with the idea, and eventually eight of us from the orchestra participated.

We had two percussionists, three brass, a bass, a guitar, and a keyboard. We decided to call the group Symphonic Metamorphosis in honor of Hindemith's famous piece that had affected me so many years ago. We would "metamorphose" into a rock and roll group like Blood Sweat and Tears, or Chicago.

We all got together one day and headed for Chicago to a big musical trade show and visited a company called Custom. We let them know we were from the Detroit Symphony Orchestra, we had no background at all in rock and roll, and we needed help. Well, Custom believed in us. They gave us guitars and amplifiers — thousands of dollars' worth of stuff. Also, the percussion company Slingerland, gave us all the percussion equipment we would ever need. We hadn't even created a repertoire yet — well, maybe one or two tunes, but it was pretty sketchy.

We started rehearsing after the DSO concerts at a little place we'd found on Woodward Avenue that we called Funky Woodward. We used the space to create and rehearse tunes and stored our equipment there. Erv Monroe created almost all the tunes. They were wonderful, we believed in ourselves.

Gradually we accumulated enough repertoire to do a concert. We got a manager from New York, and we were on our way. Other people believed in us, too, though a lot of people thought we were silly, and some resisted the idea that symphony musicians could play rock and roll.

For several of the more classical-style pieces like "Girl with the Flaxen Hair" (Debussy), we would put down the microphones, walk out into the audience, and play acoustically. Then we would go back up on stage, pick up our mikes, and rock.

Symphonic Metamorphosis
Back (left to right): Don Hoss, Dennis Smith, David Krehbiel,
Bob Pangborn. Front (left to right): Bob Cowart, Erv Monroe, Sam Tundo, Tom Bacon

Rocking with Detroit Symphony Orchestra

The Detroit Symphony Orchestra even featured our rock group. At that time, DSO was playing in Ford Auditorium, which had a pit in front of the stage. One of our rock group's main pieces started with a quote from Strauss's *Also Sprach Zarathustra*. The orchestra played the opening of *Zarathustra*, and then the pit lifted up with the band on it decked out in ruffled, quasi-classical costumes. And we'd rock! It was pretty outrageous.

We even commissioned a piece by the famous composer Donald Erb called *Klein Farben Funk* for our rock group and full symphony orchestra. We played this piece several times with the Detroit Symphony.

Symphony versus Rock

A few times, a bit of tension developed between the orchestra and Symphonic Metamorphosis. Every fall the orchestra went to Worcester, Massachusetts for the Worcester festival. One year the members of Symphonic Metamorphosis were the featured soloists. As we got off the plane, the reporters, who had been waiting for us, came up immediately to talk to us while the conductor stood by unnoticed. He was more than a little miffed about this. We were pushing the limits.

Another time as we played a concert at Ford Auditorium with the orchestra, a man in a brown suit came running down the aisle from the back of the audience, evidently offended that the symphony was playing this kind of music. He ran up onto the stage and began pulling the cords out of our amplifiers and disconnecting our microphones.

Well, the amplifiers have what is called a reverb unit, and when you disturb it, it makes a terrible crashing sound. When this guy jerked on the amplifiers the noise was horrendous, but we kept playing right through it even though we lost our mikes. Eventually I guess the guy was finally satisfied or just got tired of it, and he walked off the stage.

This sort of disturbance was quite the unusual occasion for a symphony concert, and we could hardly wait until the next day when the papers would come out with their reviews telling what they thought about it. The amazing thing was that not a word was mentioned anywhere. Evidently the Symphony had covered up the whole thing. What had been a huge event for those of us in the orchestra never became public.

Overall, we enjoyed quite a bit of success in our time as Symphonic Metamorphosis. We made two recordings for London Records. We played the Playboy club in New York City. We played the Tanglewood Festival. We even created new songs for Tanglewood, including one we called "Money Man." We threw money to the audience when we played that one.

1st Album, London Records, 33 1/3

2nd Album, London Records, 33 1/3

Are Conductors People, Too?

By this time, I'd begun to rethink my attitude about conductors — maybe some of them did have a sense of humor, and quite possibly they were real people just like us. I decided to try giving them the benefit of the doubt, and this created some enlightening moments for me.

During the time our rock group was going strong, we began having tailgate parties out in the parking lot after DSO concerts at our summer home at Meadow Brook.

When Michael Tilson Thomas came to conduct, I invited him to come and have a beer with us after one of our concerts, thinking, *He's a conductor, sure, but he's a person.* He was a young guy maybe ten years younger than I. He was thrilled to be asked and seemed just one of the guys! (Of course, I could never have done this with Reiner.)

I forgot about this incident with Michael until much later at the end of my career, when he became conductor of the San Francisco Symphony Orchestra — and my boss. He mentioned many times how much he had appreciated my hospitality and that it had left quite an impression on him.

This was a good reminder that people you meet in the music business are probably going to turn up again. If you don't treat them right, it could be tough for you down the road.

Fun at the Lake

Some of the greatest fun we had was at our cottage at Brighton on Little Crooked Lake where the whole rock group hung out. We had a wonderful camaraderie and had become the best of friends.

One time we got the idea that it would be fun to drag each other around in a big inner tube we tied to the back of the boat. I didn't participate in this particular activity but three or four of the guys did. The first guy sat on the inner tube for his ride, and when he came back, we asked how it was. "Oh, it was great!" he said, and encouraged someone else to go.

The next guy went out for his ride around the lake and came back saying, "Wow, was that fun!" And he encouraged the next guy to go. All of them seemed to be having a great time. Then the last guy to take a ride in the inner tube hit a wake that a bigger boat had made. He was pulled into the wake and then bounced off the wave when it hit him. It tore off his swimsuit and threw him into the air.

When asked what it was like, he said it was terrible, like getting hit in the butt with a sledgehammer, and that was the end of that activity.

A couple of days later we had a rock concert at Meadow Brook. As we put on our costumes, one of the guys said, "Hey! Look at this!" His whole butt was black and blue. Everyone else started saying, "Oh, yeah, look at mine!" They all showed off their bruised butts.

Funny how no one at the lake would admit that it really hurt. They just put up with it and talked the next guy into doing it.

We all learned through our rock band experience that we could do more than just play in a symphony orchestra. For one thing, I learned that I didn't need to get tired. I didn't need to take naps before concerts. We'd rent an RV, and all of us would pile in and go to a rock performance. With practically no sleep at all, we'd show up for a symphony rehearsal the next morning, and we'd be fine. Being tired was all in the mind.

I also learned that I could stand up and play a two-hour concert by memory and it was no problem. When you are in an orchestra you learn to believe in some limitations you put on yourself that you don't have to believe in. Overcoming those limitations was part of the joy of forming this group. Thank God we didn't get famous at it, though, because we'd all be drug addicts or dead by now. We were smoking and drinking a lot. But the freedom to do our own thing and create our own music led us out of the prison of playing in orchestras, especially that particular orchestra at that particular time.

The rock group gradually faded out. We all went on to other things. Our bass player/English horn player, Bob Cowart, left for the Los Angeles Philharmonic, as did our trombone player, Dennis

Bob Cowart and David Krehbiel

Smith. My friend Erv Monroe was president of a flute company and became the premier flute dealer/distributor in the country. He also wrote and published a lot of music. He was a dynamo and remained principal flute in Detroit until his retirement in 2008.

ᕙ

23. DSO MOVES TO ORCHESTRA HALL

By the early 1970s, all of us in the Detroit Symphony had become sick and tired of playing in Ford auditorium downtown on the river across from Canada. It was a big barn with no charm, an auditorium, not a concert hall.

The original Orchestra Hall in Detroit had been a beautiful building on Woodward Avenue, designed in 1919 by the famous conductor of the Detroit Symphony Orchestra, Ossip Gabrilowitsch. Financial difficulties due to the Great Depression forced DSO to move to more economical quarters.

Orchestra Hall became a neighborhood church for a time, and later, with new owners, it became a venue for jazz concerts called Paradise Theater. By the 1970s, it had been abandoned for twenty years. It was quickly deteriorating and had holes in the roof. The plan was to tear it down. But orchestra members got together, started committees, and began the process of getting the hall refurbished. Presently, the Detroit Symphony Orchestra plays in a beautiful hall, with real charm and a wonderful acoustic.

To start raising money for the renovation of the hall, we played a concert in it while it still had holes in the ceiling and pigeons flying around inside. Somehow OSHA let us play there even though it wasn't safe. Sixten Ehrling conducted this concert. What I remember most about it is that at the end of the concert when people were clapping, he went offstage and came back with a gob of something stuck to his forehead. We all thought, *Oh my God, a pigeon got him!*

Upon investigation, we found that it wasn't from a pigeon at all. He was such a voracious smoker that when he went offstage, he'd ripped open a pack of cigarettes and a bit of the cellophane stuck to his face, which was sweaty from the performance. Strange, the things you remember about a place.

DSO retirement party
From (left to right): Willard Darling, Tom Bacon,
David Krehbiel, Keith Vernon, Ed Sauve, Charlie Weaver

PART IV

❧

THE OZAWA ERA
(1972-1975)

24. Audition Mania

Once there was a young man who wanted to become an actor, so he went around asking people, "What do you do to become an actor?" Someone suggested that he find a theater company and help out backstage so he could be immersed in the environment. This he did, and all the time he studied, trying to prepare himself in case he was ever needed on stage. One night the director came to him and said, "We need you to fill in for someone who is sick." Finally, his big chance, his debut!

"What do I have to do?" he asked.

The director said, "Well, in the third act we will dress you as a soldier. When you go onstage, a cannon will go off. When you hear it, you say, "Hark, I hear the cannon!"

Excited about the prospect, he went to his dressing room, put his costume on, and began practicing the many different permutations of the line that was to mark his theater debut.

Hark! I hear the cannon!

Hark! **I** hear the cannon!

Hark! I **hear** the cannon!

Hark! I hear the **cannon!**

Finally, he decided how he was going to say it in order to make a perfect start to his acting career. There was a knock on the door.

"Okay, you're on!" a voice said.

They pushed him onstage and the cannon went off.

He screamed, "Ahhh!! What the hell was that!?!"

We practice and practice and think we are prepared. But we aren't really prepared. We have no idea what it will feel like or what will occur once we go out on that stage for a five-minute audition that is the culmination of years of study and practice. Getting ready for an audition requires more than just knowing the notes and the black marks on the page. You never know what surprise might await you onstage. You have to be prepared physically, mentally, and emotionally.

Playing in the Present

The key for me is to occupy my mind with the emotion the composer is communicating in the passage I am playing. This, in turn, keeps my thoughts of what might happen before and after the audition or performance at bay. When I am in the present, playing how I feel musically right now, it's one of the most conscious, most alive times I can have. (Appendix A)

Auditioning in San Francisco

After thinking I would spend the rest of my career in Detroit, I left in 1972 for a job as principal horn with the San Francisco Symphony Orchestra. My wife and I really wanted to get back to California, but we never thought we'd have the chance. Then the opportunity in San Francisco came up. Once again the door opened and I was able to walk through it.

I had auditioned for the San Francisco Symphony Orchestra once before, in 1956 while I was a junior at Fresno State College. I'd heard about an opening for the fourth horn chair in the orchestra, and since I considered myself a pretty good horn player by that time, I decided to give it a try. I played for the principal horn Ross Taylor. He said to me, "Hey, kid, you're not ready for this!"

Now, fifteen years later in 1972, the principal horn job became available in San Francisco. I couldn't resist signing up to audition.

I had nine years' experience playing principal horn in Detroit, but I'd never had to face the kind of audition experience evolving at that time where 70 or 80 candidates auditioned before an audition committee. Up to that point I'd only played for personnel managers and music directors. So it was really a new experience for me, and I was nervous.

Again, the doors opened. Not only was there a principal horn position open in San Francisco, but another opened with the Boston Symphony Orchestra. I decided that I would audition in Boston as well as San Francisco, not because I cared about playing in the Boston Symphony, but because using the experience as a practice audition might improve my chances for success in San Francisco.

The audition in Boston was a relatively small affair. I played for the interim musical director, William Steinberg, and a committee onstage at Symphony Hall in Boston. Shortly afterward, I received notice that Charles Kavalovski and I were in a tie for the position and that we were invited to come back and play with the orchestra so they could choose between us.

But I wasn't interested in going to Boston. Soon I would be traveling to the audition in San Francisco. The moment I got on the plane from Detroit to San Francisco, I had a feeling of déja vù — this job was mine, and this was our time to get back to California.

In San Francisco — and this was the experience of most players now — I joined a room full of candidates warming up and preparing to audition. Charles Kavalovski, with whom I had tied in Boston, was among them.

San Francisco's contract included a clause that said if the orchestra offered an audition candidate a job, the candidate had to accept or decline on the spot. This was probably the orchestra's reaction to being pushed around by auditioners who were trying to leave room to negotiate further, or who were waiting to see how they did in another audition. But the contract put a stop to that by spelling out the conditions — here's the job; here's the salary; you've got to say *yes* or *no*, right now.

After playing the audition, we all waited together backstage at the Opera House for the results, sitting around on top of bass cases strewn about for what seemed like forever. I felt sure I had played at least as well as Kavalovski had played. Also, I felt so certain that the job was mine.

Finally the manager came in and I thought, *well, finally, he's coming to call me.* To my horror, he passed me by and beckoned Kavalovski, who followed him to a dressing room offstage somewhere. In a few minutes Kavalovski walked back past me, scowling, and said, "Why don't you just stay out of my life!" I don't remember what I said back to him, but I was busy with my own life at the moment and certainly didn't feel as though I was in his.

Kavalovski left, and the manager motioned me into the room. Kavalovski and I hadn't tied this time, but we were only a few points apart, and it had taken the committee quite a while to decide between us. They had chosen Kavalovski, but because of the stipulation about saying *yes* or *no* on the spot, Kavalovski had to tell them that he couldn't accept the job because he was a finalist in the Boston audition.

They explained the whole thing to me and asked if I would accept the job for the salary offered. I said, "Where do I sign?" So Chuck Kavalovski and I both ended up getting what we wanted. We've since become friends. He spent many years playing principal horn in the Boston Symphony Orchestra and is now retired, too.

On Practicing

Chuck and I were different in that he practiced every day and had a routine he followed, while I wasn't much interested in practicing. I'd do just enough to get by. I'd play a little and if things didn't feel

free or weren't working properly I'd try to understand why and fix it right there.

I always thought it would be weird to carry my horn around everywhere. I know people who take their horns on backpacking trips! They couldn't go a day without playing, and I was never like that. In fact, more and more as my hornplaying developed,

I realized it was essential for me to take two or three weeks off after the symphony season each year.

Towards the end of each season it became harder for me to feel free in my playing. As each season progressed, I think I developed some bad habits that detracted from my ease of playing. I found that if I took two to three weeks off in August and then began to play again when the season started, I would have a fresh start without all the bad habits.

During the summers, our family would spend time at a cabin Carol's parents owned at Huntington Lake. I'd play my horn out on the porch over an open area like I did in Yosemite when I was in college. Two or three days of that and I was ready to go again.

Playing out under the trees and into open spaces, not in a hotel or in a room, is a good idea for any horn player. It encourages efficiency and the right attitude about what the horn is supposed to be for. The horn originated as an instrument to be played outside to rally hunting parties.

I have always said that I was the best player in the country. It was only in the city that I had trouble sometimes.

At Home in San Francisco

We could hardly wait to move back to California! As soon as the San Francisco Symphony offered me the job as principal horn, we bought a brand new Dodge van — a Tradesman model with windows on only one side. We had the idea that it wouldn't be so hot in the car in the California heat. My friend conductor Henry Lewis laughed and laughed when I told him about this design feature. He said, "But you'll only see half the country!"

The orchestra paid for moving most of our stuff. We packed the rest — plus the dog — in our new van, and headed out for California, singing "California, here we come" all the way.

We bought a home in a beautiful setting in Mill Valley, just north of San Francisco, for $56,000 — way over our budget! But it was a perfect place to raise our two children, Kristin, who was 10, and Art, 7.

Behind our house was an abandoned railroad track going through an abandoned tunnel, with woods lining the far side of the track. The grade school, junior high, and high school were an easy walk down the tracks, which later became a bike path.

Kristin was horse-crazy, and still is. One might call her a "horse-whisperer." She began training horses and riders when she was very young. We boarded her horse at Tennessee Valley along the Marin seashore. On occasion we kept the horse in a corral in the woods behind our house. Years later, Kristin told us that one day while we were at work and she was at home by herself not feeling well, she'd become lonely and brought the horse into the house to keep her company.

Kristin married a cowboy named Lee Hall. Today they raise horses and train them as well as their riders. Many of her clients bring horses to her that they have had trouble controlling. But with Kristin, the horse stands still as she mounts, and then obeys as she rides away with perfect ease.

Kristin's way of training clients on their horses reminds me of how I teach students to play the horn. She teaches them how to be conscious of the dynamics between themselves and their horse, then to relax and ride with that consciousness in mind at all moments. This is not unlike how I try to play and teach the horn.

In 1972 the railroad tracks behind our house were still in place. I made a cart that I rode down to the bay on those abandoned tracks. People would stop and gawk at me as I rumbled across Camino Alto and down the tracks on my cart.

Later, when the tracks became a bike path, I made a cart that I could pull with my bike to haul my canoe down to the bay. Eventually I would use this same path to bike to my 7 a.m. AA meetings. Because we had easy access to the fire roads leading to Mt. Tamalpais, I became interested in bicycles. I was one of the first to put derailleurs on fat-tired bikes for the steep climb up Mt. Tam.

I was crazy about motorcycles, and one of the most exciting things I did when we moved back to California was to buy my first motorcycle — or I should say I bought several over a period of time. I kept one in Mill Valley for the half-hour commute to work across Golden Gate Bridge to the Opera House, dressed in complete paraphernalia — boots, jacket, helmet, gloves, and my horn strapped to my back. The other motorcycles I rode when we visited our farm in Reedley. I'm proud to say, though, I never owned a Harley.

〜

———— 25. SEIJI OZAWA ————

Seiji Ozawa, the San Francisco Symphony conductor who hired me, was the most physically elegant conductor I have ever worked for. His conducting movements hypnotized both the orchestra and his audiences. No one looked better when conducting than Seiji.

There was something missing, though. Playing for him and watching him as an audience member was always exciting. But hearing his performances on the radio or on recordings without the visual effect was always disappointing.

Herbert Blomstedt was two conductors later than Seiji in the chronology of San Francisco Symphony music directors. If you compared their recordings, Blomstedt's interpretations sounded better and made more sense than Seiji's. Though Blomstedt looked really awkward when he conducted, his tempos and emotional interpretations were right on. Compared to Blomstedt's performances, Seiji's seemed a little off. There was something missing; or maybe there was something from his Japanese culture that didn't quite translate to our Western music.

Seiji was charming and charismatic. He had an incredible memory and an incredible talent, and he never used a score. When he talked, Seiji spoke pidgin English with a heavy Japanese accent.

Early Horn Section in San Francisco Symphony Orchestra
Left to right: Bruce Roberts, Bob Ward, Jerry Merrill, Ralph Hotz,
Lori Westin, David Krehbiel

Some people told me this was a put-on and that if you caught him at the right time he could speak perfect English. I never got a chance to find out if that was true. In the orchestra, our workplace banter included a lot of "Seiji-isms."

Seiji loved to ski. He'd take off on Sundays and Mondays for the slopes. You could always tell when he had been skiing. When he came in on Tuesdays he looked like a raccoon because his goggles had left fresh white circles around the eyes, and his beautiful brown skin was even browner.

After ten years or so with an orchestra, all conductors seem to wear thin, and they have to move on. I didn't have the chance to get tired of Seiji. He was with SFO only two years after I was hired. Then he went to the Boston Symphony where he stayed for many years.

Faking It

One of my first experiences with Seiji was the Haydn Symphony No. 51, which requires the horns to play in the extreme high register. The highest note in the piece is a written F about a fourth higher than the horn is usually expected to play.

That note was really out of my range, and I didn't know how I was going to play it. Bob Lambert, the principal trombone in Chicago, used to say, *Those notes are so high that they have snow on them year-round.* I looked at the music and wondered if I should try a different mouthpiece.

Years ago, at Northwestern, I was discovering how resonance inside the mouth worked, and how a higher resonant frequency could make the higher notes on the horn more achievable. My mouth has a high roof with two deep grooves in it, creating a deeper resonant frequency. This is probably why I sounded so dark when I played on the trumpet.

As an experiment, I had a dentist take an impression of the inside of my mouth and make a clear plastic plate that fit into the top of my mouth and flattened out those two grooves in the upper palate, thus forming a higher resonant frequency.

Boy, could I screech high notes then! The other notes didn't sound very good, but I couldn't play the high notes without that device. I would never use it in a concert, though. So my dilemma was to figure how to resonate the high written F in Haydn's 51st without it. I experimented and experimented and finally I realized that I wasn't going to reach that high F without hurting myself.

Strangely enough, in my experiments I discovered that I could sing those high F's in a falsetto, and that if I sang them through the horn they sounded like I was playing them. So instead of vibrating my lips at the frequency of those high notes I vibrated my vocal cords in a falsetto. No one knows how a horn is supposed to sound when it's up that high anyway. What did I have to lose? It was better than hurting myself trying to hit the notes unsuccessfully. So I sang them. When I look back at this I think I must have been crazy!

At our first rehearsal of the Haydn, we sat onstage waiting to rehearse. Seiji came out and said to me in his pidgin English, "Ahh, you! Can you play those notes?"

"Yeah, would you like to hear them?" I asked.

"Ahh, yeh!" he said.

So I played this passage and sang the top note. He said, "Very good, very good!" So that whole week during rehearsals and concerts

I sang those top notes every time. No one knew it except my friends. They were all laughing.

I always likened Haydn 51 to Area 51, the secret base for UFOs in Nevada. Haydn 51 is the Area 51 of horn players.

In this business sometimes you just have to figure out a way to make it happen. Anything goes. One of the tricks we'd use was in Beethoven's Fourth Symphony, which has a pianissimo entrance on a high concert E-flat. It's very exposed and treacherous. We figured out a way to take out a tuning slide, and through the resulting opening, play the concert D immediately below that E-flat inaudibly. Right before the entrance in Beethoven's 4th, we would play the D along with the bassoon, then just push the valve down and the inaudible D would slip right up into a beautiful high E-flat.

To Japan with Seiji

We went on tour to Japan with Seiji. The Japanese were thrilled at having one of their own conducting a major orchestra from the United States. Our visit to Japan generated a lot of local publicity, and it had been arranged that we would play on national television.

The program was the ballet *Daphnis and Chloe*, the longest of Maurice Ravel's works. With its lush harmonies typical of the impressionist movement, the piece has some interesting high notes for the horn. I was worried. Any time you play on live television you don't want to have a disaster. Fortunately, the concert went well and was a big success.

The next morning we had a rehearsal for the next concert. With his broken English, Seiji couldn't make an "L" sound. When he came onstage he said to us, "Ahh! Very good concert! You pray and pray and pray, and the audience they crap and crap and crap!" We all roared. He, of course, didn't understand what we were laughing about, and said, "Ahh! Seiji made funny!"

In Japan, my friends and I collected temple bells and took them into the resonant stairwell in the hotel to play after the concerts. I still use mine at home for meditation.

In my tenure of 25 years in San Francisco, I saw the orchestra go from mediocre to world class. It's not that Seiji was bad, it's just that he didn't have much to work with when he arrived. Turnover of players and conductors over the years and the change in the auditioning process helped fuel the orchestra's artistic growth.

It helped now that an audition committee appointed from the orchestra decided on one candidate out of an auditioning field of 70 or 80 players, rather than the music director alone making a choice from only one or two candidates. Increased activity of the unions meant better working conditions and better pay for the musicians. The orchestra committee also had some say in who was hired as the conductor.

Over the years I played with the Chicago and Detroit symphonies, I made great strides in my pursuit of ease of playing and the attitude of Creative Not Caring. Now I could spend most of my 25 years with San Francisco enjoying the music and having fun with it, or at least being able to accept whatever happened.

Critics

Shortly after I began with the San Francisco Symphony Orchestra, I played the Britten Serenade for Tenor, Horn, and Strings, which I would do several more times over my 25 years there. The Serenade calls for an opening solo on natural horn; that is, a horn without valves. I always used my Geyer natural horn to play the Prologue and the Epilogue, and I've always believed that when playing these movements, you shouldn't try to play completely in tune but should allow the eleventh partial of the harmonic series to be a little sharp, just as it occurs naturally (see Appendix D). This adds a wonderful grating flavor.

When I played it the first time in San Francisco, I used this approach and got two reviews which were polar opposites. One review was really derogatory, saying that Krehbiel completely ruined the concert by playing out of tune. The other review said, "The opening of the Britten Serenade alone was worth the price of the concert."

I cut these reviews out and put them up in my office so I could look at them and be reminded that everything was a matter of opinion. Music critics love to hear a missed note on the horn so they can write a whole review about it, as if to say, *What a wonderful ear I have, I heard this one mistake!* But if I pat myself on the back about the good reviews I get, I also have to accept that the bad ones are just as valid.

We can't run our lives worrying about music critics. In the end, I have to be my own reviewer. Keeping this attitude helps relieve performance anxiety and promote ease of playing.

Taking Chances

Being able to enjoy the music and having fun with it didn't mean I never made errors. Nor did it mean I was always right about everything I taught. I was a featured artist at an international horn workshop in Potsdam, New York, in 1988 where I met Frank Lloyd. We were both soloists, and our studios were right next to each other. One day I ran into Frank as I came out of my studio buzzing my mouthpiece. Frank asked me what I was doing.

"I'm buzzing my mouthpiece," I said, "making sure everything's working right."

He said, "Huh, I never heard of such a thing." He took out his mouthpiece and tried to buzz on it. It was awful. I thought, *Oh, my God! This poor guy! How's he going to play the horn?*

Well, at the concert that night he was incredible! So I had to rethink all my theories about buzzing because either he was just putting me on that he couldn't buzz, or he couldn't buzz but could play like a god.

I had one of my career's most embarrassing moments at that workshop. One of the pieces I played on my solo recital was "He Was Despised," an alto solo from the *Messiah*. I always push my students to take chances, to try new things, lest they get stuck in old ways of doing things when a new way might work better. However the reverse can happen, and did happen to me with this beautiful solo from the *Messiah*.

I began playing this song, feeling totally in the moment. It's a lovely song on the horn, in just the right range. In the song, the words "despised" and "rejected" are sung over three syllables and are written for the same three notes in succession. But when I got to "despised" for the first statement of the figure, I decided on the spur of the moment that when the figure returned for "rejected," I would play it on stopped horn.

This I did, except I managed to mis-transpose the stopped horn notes for "rejected." What came out wasn't even close to what was written, and of course, it sounded terrible! I got the award for the best clam in that workshop because of those three notes. So much for spontaneity!

\~\~

26. HORN MESSIAH

I had begun doing quite a few workshops as both soloist and conductor. In 1972, my first year with the San Francisco Symphony Orchestra, I got the idea of transcribing a few choruses from the *Messiah* for horn choir and soloists. I wasn't really a capable arranger, so I presented this idea to a former student of mine, Jim DeCorsey, who was teaching at Lawrence University in Appleton, Wisconsin.

Jim combined his arranging skills with my ideas and came up with a wonderful arrangement of several pieces from the *Messiah*. The arrangement called for a massive horn choir of 100 to 200 players for the choruses and a group of six soloists in front to play the orchestra parts.

I conducted this work in its premiere at an International Horn Society workshop some years later. It worked just great for a horn workshop and a mass horn choir. Strangely, the horn choir sounded like a singing choir, just an amazing sound.

The sixth solo voice part was very low and hard to project, so sometimes I'd have a tuba player come in and play that part. I'd introduce the tuba player as the "bass French horn player" whose arm wasn't long enough to get into the bell. It was thrilling to conduct this piece and make it work.

This performance was the first time I experienced what it was like to be a conductor. I felt isolated, like I was on an island with no one around me. At the reception afterwards I felt like I was *persona non grata*. No one interacted with me at all. I kept thinking that since the concert had been such a success someone would come up to say *Wow! Congratulations!*, but it didn't happen. I started doubting myself — maybe the performance wasn't so good after all? So this was how it felt to be a conductor!

About the only praise I got that night came from James Chambers, the famous horn player who had retired as principal horn of the New York Philharmonic, and to whose honor that year's workshop had been dedicated. He came up to me afterward and said, "That was the most wonderful thing I've ever heard from a horn choir." He said it was the first time he'd heard a group of that many horn players make music, and told me he would tell my conductor, Edo de Waart, what a great thing I did.

That helped make up for feeling totally ignored, but I'll always remember my first experience of what it was like to be on the dark side, where the players can't like the conductor.

〜

27. BREATH CONTROL

Return of Henry Lewis

Conductor and vocal coach Henry Lewis, whom I met when I was in Detroit playing the children's concerts and who was responsible for my having to learn new techniques for endurance while playing horn in the Mendelssohn *Nocturne,* stayed at our home when he conducted the San Francisco Opera.

We'd become friends with both Henry and his wife, opera singer Marilyn Horne. Their daughter Angela and our son Art were close in age, so we had some family get-togethers.

Whenever Henry stayed with us, the two of us played records, drank, and talked about music late into the night.

One night, after who knows how many drinks, we started talking about playing and singing. Henry was a wonderful vocal coach. He coached his wife as well as many other fine singers. He knew a lot about tone production in singing. We talked about similarities between playing the horn and singing, and we realized that singing with the right kind of resonance and freedom, without effort, was a lot like the "ease of playing" approach I'd developed for the horn.

After we discussed this for a while, I said, "Well, Henry, why don't you play my horn?" I had a horn right there and handed it to him. He had never played a horn before. But just by understanding the principles we talked about — vocal production and how the embouchure works — he played right up to high C with a great sound. I was absolutely amazed.

After playing the horn, Henry said, "Okay, now it's your turn. Let's hear you sing." So I sang. I am a tenor, the kind of tenor whose voice fails after about three minutes. I get tired, and then my voice doesn't work anymore. But that night, I sang up to some high notes in a voice I've never heard come out of myself before. I felt totally uninhibited, just like Henry had been with the horn. I've tried to duplicate whatever happened that night, but I've not been able to do it again with my singing.

Karl Smith

When I think of working with Henry in Detroit and having my endurance challenged when he conducted the Mendelssohn *Nocturne,* I am reminded of how I came to meet Karl Smith.

A friend of mine in the Chicago Symphony Orchestra, Frank Kaderabek, kept telling me about a trombone player he knew from California named Karl Smith. Frank knew Karl from his days in the Dallas Symphony, and insisted I had to meet him sometime when I was in California. He said Karl was an inventor and an interesting man who owned a dude ranch somewhere near Yosemite.

I moved back to California and forgot all about Karl Smith. Each year, Carol and I and our two kids spent two weeks camping with another family in the high Sierra. One afternoon I was playing my horn out on a granite slab when an older man approached me. It turned out to be Karl Smith, the man I had heard about several years before.

Having similar backgrounds and a friend in common, we became friends almost instantly. His dude ranch was about three miles above Florence Lake and only a mile from the famous John Muir Trail. The only way to get to his ranch was to take a ferry boat across the lake and hike the three miles. Our campsite was just below the lake at Jackass Meadow.

Karl happened to be passing by on a supply trip for his dude ranch and heard me playing out on the rock slab. Right then and there, he gave me important advice about breath support. When Karl was a young man, he had studied with Herbert L. Clark, the famous cornet soloist who in turn had studied with the famous singer Enrico Caruso. So Karl's advice could be said to come from Caruso himself!

Here it is: as you play, push gently outward from the navel area, and you will remove tension from the middle part of the body. As a result, the middle body becomes inert like the "u" part of a magnet, and you have a positive pole at the embouchure, a negative pole at the navel, and a tension-free area between those two poles.

I was amazed at the synchronicity of meeting Karl on that slab of rock and getting advice passed down from the mouth of Caruso — another door opens!

◦

—— 28. THE OPERA HOUSE ——

I loved playing operas and I loved the San Francisco Opera House! Built in the 1930's, the Opera House is connected to War Memorial Auditorium by a tunnel running underneath the court-yard. My friends from the orchestra and I liked to go exploring in the tunnel. We'd call it "going down to the river" because along one side of the tunnel was a concrete drainage ditch with a little stream of water running through it. This was "the river."

We'd explore all over the Opera House, clear up into the attic where rooms were filled with old opera props — spears, swords, and costumes. From the attic we could climb down into the giant chandelier in the middle of the concert hall. I suppose access to the chandelier was provided not for our amusement, but so that maintenance people could change light bulbs and such.

Our exploring led us to the roof where there was a wonderful view. One of the explorers sat on a skylight and broke a glass pane. Now, of course, rainwater could drip down onto the stage. We wondered what we should do. We certainly couldn't tell anyone.

A couple of days later I realized that the sun was in just the right position during rehearsals to shine a shaft of light through the hole in the otherwise opaque glass and onto the stage. We were relieved to know that someone responsible for maintenance would become aware of the hole and go up to fix it without us having to admit that we caused it.

The War Memorial Building, attached to the Opera House, was where the first United Nations met after the Second World War. There's a lot of history in those old buildings.

When I first started in San Francisco in 1972, the Opera Orchestra and the Symphony Orchestra shared the same players but had different managements. The Opera would perform in the fall and then the same players would play in the Symphony when its season started later.

When Edo de Waart became the new conductor of the Symphony a few years later, there was a big push to separate the Opera from the Symphony, so they built Davies Symphony Hall. Then the players of the Opera and Symphony had to choose between the two orchestras. Some of the players decided to stay with the Opera. Some of us went with the Symphony.

A lot of new players came into the Symphony to fill the positions vacated by players who chose to stay with the Opera. I really missed the Opera though. There was nothing like playing with the Opera. It was always exciting.

In the Opera at that time, the horns sat at the edge of the orchestra in the pit right next to the audience. Older ladies would often come in, throw their fur coats over the railing, and take their seats in the front row. Often I had to brush aside a fur coat dangling in my face.

But I've always said that sitting right where the performance meets the audience is like being at the seashore where the ocean meets the land — it's an incredibly powerful spot. From this vantage point, the singers were larger than life, singing right down on us. It was much unlike our usual seating in the pit with the horns in the back of the orchestra where sometimes we were under the stage and missed seeing the soloists at all while they performed.

This brings to mind the old adage orchestra musicians have used forever. Question: What is the difference between a bull and an orchestra? Answer: With an orchestra, the horns are in the back.

Wagner's *Parsifal* was the first opera I ever played with the San Francisco Opera. The performance left a huge impression on me. Kurt Moll, who played Gurnemanz, sang with an effortless freedom in a tireless baritone voice that filled the opera house for hours at a time. I wondered how I could emulate that on the horn.

Opera could be both serious and humorous. But with conductors like Christof Perick, it was best to err to the side of serious. We played Wagner's opera *The Flying Dutchman*, with Perick, who came from Germany as guest conductor. I heard that his real name was Prick, but in order to avoid the unsavory connotations of such a name when conducting in an English-speaking country he had to add an "e", so that it became Perick.

During the rehearsal he stopped the orchestra, looking behind me at third horn player Jerry Merrill, and said, "I want those notes short!"

Jerry said, "You mean like this?" He played them with exaggerated shortness — *peck, peck, peck, peck*. Perick said, "Yes, like that!"

I could almost hear Jerry roll his eyes behind me as he said, "Why?!"

"Why" is something you never ask your conductor, particularly one with no sense of humor and an authentic name of "Prick."

When something like this happened in a rehearsal, the safest course of action was to duck down behind the music stands. We called this "going to periscope depth."

This reminds me of another German-born conductor/pianist, Christoph Eschenbach, who performed with us and guest-conducted several times. He spoke in a heavy German accent and always wore a black turtleneck. We used to say that he liked conducting in San Francisco because he could park his submarine in the bay.

Seriously. . .

The famous opera conductor Karl Böhm came to San Francisco to conduct Strauss's *Die Frau ohne Schatten* (*The Woman without a Shadow*), a very serious German opera with a very serious German conductor.

I've never forgotten the level of tension in those rehearsals. In the middle of one of the most somber pieces in the opera we heard a most unmusical stirring and shuffling from somewhere back in the woodwind section, followed by a burst of laughter. The conductor stopped the music at once, glaring at the offending group. Very sternly, he said in his German accent, "Vat iss com-i-cal!?" Opera was no laughing matter for him!

—29. CREATIVE NOT CARING—

Heinz and Ursula Zimmerman

One evening while the symphony was still playing at the Opera House with Seiji, I got word that someone wanted to meet me after the concert. I went out into the hall and met a man who introduced himself as Heinz Zimmerman from Thun, Switzerland and explained that he was an amateur horn player finishing up his medical degree at the University of California in San Francisco. He and his wife, Ursula, had attended the concert, and he was wondering if I might have time in my schedule to give him a few horn lessons. It didn't take long before I realized that we were going to be best friends.

At this time, my children Kristin and Art were learning to ski. Carol and I figured that if our kids were going to learn to ski, we might as well learn, too. So when I had a couple days off we went up to Tahoe and tried skiing, but we soon realized that we needed lessons. I thought of Heinz being from Switzerland and asked him if he skied. "All the time," he said.

"I have an idea," I said, "why don't we trade lessons? You give me skiing lessons and I'll give you horn lessons." He liked that idea, and off we went to the slopes.

The interesting thing to me was the similarity between the skiing lessons and the horn lessons. When Heinz took his first horn lesson, he was tense. My first lesson for him was, "Heinz, just relax!"

When I stood looking out from the top of a hill over the slopes, I was a ball of tension. His lesson for me was, "Dave, just relax!" Same lessons. In both our cases it was the fear of future outcomes that made us tense. The cure was Creative Not Caring.

While Heinz and Ursula were living in San Francisco, we took them 200 miles south to our farm in Reedley to meet my mother and Carol's parents.

Like Heinz and Ursula, my mother was of Swiss ancestry. Her native dialect was Schweizerdeutsch, which turned out to be the same dialect Heinz and his wife Ursula spoke. What a coincidence that out of so many dialects they would speak the same one. The three of them began to jabber happily in Schweizerdeutsch, the language of my mother's childhood. I didn't know when I had seen her so happy.

My mother's grandparents and other relatives had settled in Ohio after leaving Switzerland. They spoke only Schweizerdeutsch.

My mother was born in Ohio and spoke only Schweizerdeutsch until she started elementary school. The family remained close-knit, and after marrying my father and moving to California, my mother had remained permanently homesick for Ohio and her family there.

Now my mother became good friends with Heinz and Ursula, even traveling to their home in Switzerland to visit them. Her dialect amused them because it was old-fashioned. Languages change. It was the same with Carol's Finnish grandmother. People would come to visit from Finland just to listen to her speak. They wanted to hear the old Finnish language as it was 90 years ago.

Heinz was a surgeon, the head of the emergency unit in a huge Bern hospital. These days he is retired from medicine but he still plays his horn as an amateur in the World's Doctors Orchestra, an orchestra consisting of doctors from around the world who meet once a year to play a concert in a large city in the US or Europe.

With Heinz and Ursula Zimmerman in Switzerland.

One year they met and played in San Francisco and I coached their brass section on Mahler's First Symphony. They weren't that bad considering they were doctors and not musicians.

A couple of years ago Carol and I travelled to Switzerland on a river cruise and visited the Zimmermans. I coached Heinz on his hornplaying again but there was no talk of skiing.

Heinz Zimmerman had a huge impact on our family. We had many fun times together in the snow during the winters.

Lee Hall

Later on I had the opportunity to take our son-in-law, Lee, to the slopes for his first time skiing. Lee is the cowboy who married our daughter, Kristin. He made quick progress and by the end of the day he was skiing quite well.

When I asked him how he was able to learn so fast, he said, "Falling in the snow is nothing like getting bucked off a bull or horse." With no fear of falling, he could relax and let his body take over, like learning to ride a bicycle — or learning to play the horn.

Art

Our son, Art, began a career influenced by our times skiing with Heinz. After graduating from high school Art moved straight to Tahoe. There he and a friend started a business sponsored by Squaw Valley using trick photography to make photos and videos of skiers who wanted mementos of their ski trips.

Dressed in their skier's clothing, Art and his friend had photos and videos made while they did tricks like jumping, moguls, etc., on their skis. At a distance, no one could see the faces clearly.

Then the travelers could take these photos and videos back home and show their friends what great skiers they had become at Squaw Valley.

That job morphed into going on the local radio station and giving weather reports for skiers.

Next, he and another friend started a film company called Fall Line Films, filming extreme snowboard sports from helicopters. Traveling to places like Europe and South America, they made quite a few movies of skiers doing extreme tricks like jumping over buses on snowboards.

Snowboards morphed into wakeboards, big flat boards that you ski on like a surfboard behind a boat, jumping over the wakes. For this they filmed in Florida.

Now Art is a blacksmith, although he tells me he still skis about 120 days a year. He lives only 10 minutes from Sugar Bowl ski area. He and a friend have formed a company that makes ornamental iron for railings and banisters and the like for high-end homes being built in Truckee, near Lake Tahoe.

ᘛ

30. TOURING RUSSIA WITH SEIJI

In 1975 the San Francisco Symphony went on tour to Russia with Seiji Ozawa. Russian audiences greeted us warmly and the tour was a big success. However, we were in the middle of the Cold War and conditions in Russia were austere. Outside the concert hall we were uncomfortable. The accommodations were poor, and the food was terrible. The Russian government viewed us with suspicion.

I went with a bass player friend to visit Lenin's tomb. We called him "Lenny." Forbidding signs along the way warned in English and other languages that no photographs were permitted.

We'd been waiting a long time in a long line to view Lenin and his tomb, when suddenly I noticed that my friend was gone. He had been standing behind me a moment before, but when I turned to make a comment he wasn't there.

Someone in the group who spoke English noticed my concern and told me that the guards evidently had spotted a bulge in my friend's coat pocket and whisked him away quickly for questioning. He was gone all afternoon. I didn't see him again until that night. Fortunately, they let him go in time for the concert.

When I asked him what had happened, he answered that he'd had a camera in his pocket. Yes, he'd read the signs, but he hadn't paid any attention to them.

We were in Russia for a few days and then traveled to Vilnius, Lithuania, which was like heaven in comparison. Lithuania was green and the food and accommodations were great. We all felt like we'd escaped from terrible oppression.

In the afternoon we were walking along, looking at the city and seeing the sights, when we came to a park not too far from the hotel. We were enjoying the park's lush greenness when someone called, "Look at the pot!" We looked down and found that the lush plants growing next to the sidewalk were indeed marijuana.

Oh, my God! Lithuania really *was* heaven! Well, we couldn't take pot along with us on tour. We couldn't travel with it. And we certainly couldn't take it back into Russia. So what were we to do with all this marijuana growing right next to our feet?

We decided to send a detail out late at night to pick some of the plants and bring them back to the hotel, where we dried the leaves over a lightbulb. Then we made a pipe out of a 35mm film container and a cigar tube. That night, after the concert in Vilnius, we partied! We smoked the stuff and got really giggly. It was such fun.

After half an hour or 45 minutes we began to realize that no one was getting high, and that what we had discovered in the park was industrial hemp which had none of the psychoactive properties of marijuana. We were high only because we thought we were. Strangely enough, the next morning we all woke up with sore throats. Not wanting to get caught with our improvised pipe, we dumped it down the elevator shaft.

— 31. SOLO PERFORMANCES —

Whenever I was asked to perform a solo with an orchestra, I felt honored to be invited, and I always accepted. I'd practiced the attitude of Creative Not Caring since my audition with Fritz Reiner years ago. Now, rather than imagining myself in a traffic accident so I wouldn't have to perform, I couldn't wait to get there.

Old thoughts — such as, *This seemed like a good idea at the time* — did go through my mind as performance time approached. Walking onstage right before the first notes was the scariest part. But for the most part I became tremendously present and alive during a performance, often feeling as though I was composing as I played.

Simon Rattle and Hindemith

One of my most memorable times as a soloist was with the young conductor Simon Rattle, who guest conducted the San Francisco Symphony when we performed the Hindemith Horn Concerto.

During his stay in San Francisco, we invited him to our home for dinner, and he shared some of his strategies for succeeding in his goals. He said that he had mapped out his career and was careful to accept only the assignments he felt ready to take, and that he would never conduct a piece he didn't know thoroughly.

This approach certainly paid off on his road to a very successful career, culminating with the musical directorship of the famous Berlin Philharmonic. As for me, I was in heaven again. I was playing the Hindemith Horn Concerto!

Of course, horn players are in heaven whenever they're recording or performing the big three, which are Bruckner, Mahler, and Strauss. But for me, Hindemith was right in there with them. When I played Hindemith I'd get the same feeling as when I played Mahler or Wagner. The horn became the guts of the orchestra.

There is something especially satisfying about supplying that depth of sound as a horn player. The sound of massed horns or massed Wagner tubas can dominate the whole orchestra. If you are addicted to that sound, then Hindemith, Bruckner, Mahler, and Strauss are your drugs of choice. I might also add Brahms to that list.

Lip Trilling

At the other end of the scale, I loved the lighter sound (but much greater challenge) of lip trilling.

I learned at Northwestern that lip trilling was a matter of making an extreme connection between the notes next to each other in the harmonic series by playing into the center of a note until it pops up to the next partial. Any pulling back in the efficiency or core of the note makes lip trilling impossible.

Mahler Four is a good example of a piece featuring lip trills, but sometime in the 1980s, Barry Tuckwell sent me a copy of the music for the Leopold Mozart Concerto, which is an absolute orgy of them. This became my go-to piece to perform for any masterclass or workshop. Greg Hustis, the principal horn of the Dallas Symphony, heard me play it and told me later that he thought if I could play it he could play it, too. He went on to record it commercially.

ᴎ

——— 32. FOR HORN ALONE ———

I taught for a time at the Barry Tuckwell Institute in Colorado. For the last recital of the institute, I asked Barry if he would perform a piece I had written. He agreed and asked me for the music. I said, "There is no music!" He said, "Well, what do I have to do?"

I said, "All you have to do is take a horn out onto the stage and set it on a chair."

The piece was called "For Horn Alone."

Performance of the piece required that the audience members close their eyes and meditate on the essence of the horn, its physical beauty, its beautiful sound, and its fantastic history — truly a piece for horn alone.

Once I had a girlfriend who was an Elvis fan. I couldn't understand what she saw in that kind of music. It didn't make any sense to me. Maybe I was being a bit of a snob, but I had always related to the world only through classical music. In hindsight I can better see the appeal of other musical styles. Recently I watched a country music extravaganza on Public Television with Ken Burns, and I started thinking that I might have missed a lot.

I was never what you'd call a horn jock, either. Sometimes at workshops I would see people wearing belts with horn insignias on them! I never got into that. Once when I was in the Chicago Symphony Orchestra on tour, we visited a principal horn player in Detroit whose home was full of horn lamps and horn clocks — horn stuff everywhere! I never felt that way about the instrument. The horn was just my way into the music.

If I ever achieved any kind of understanding of how to play the horn, it didn't come from being better than anyone else. For me, getting better and more comfortable on the horn was a matter of survival whenever I went through another of the doors that opened to me.

I really was pretty lazy about practicing until push came to shove and I found I'd gotten myself into the Chicago Symphony

Orchestra somehow by raw instinct. Once there, I had to figure out how to survive and keep myself comfortable. This meant controlling my nerves so I could play consistently at a certain level and not have bad days. It meant realizing that playing to my potential required me to look past my ego and express what was in my soul.

I feel fortunate that I was able to define a niche that worked for me. What would have happened had I been born in a different place or a different era? The timing was right and the right doors appeared for me to walk through.

Horns I've Owned

I have owned and played many different horns. I've never been very loyal to any one brand. Most people say I sound the same no matter what brand of horn I'm playing at the moment. I don't know whether this is good or bad.

My first horn was a Bucher, which was a copy of the Conn 6D. When I got to Chicago, everyone had Geyers. So I went up to Carl Geyer's shop on Wabash Avenue to ask about buying a horn. He heard me play a few notes and said my tone was thin, so he would make a horn for me with a larger throated bell to fix my sound. I kept that horn for some years but eventually sold it because I felt I could not make smooth slurs with it.

Sitting next to Farkas in the Symphony, I started playing the new Holton horn that he had helped design, even though when anything came up that Farkas was worried about, he would put down his new Holton and bring out his old Conn 8D.

Many years later I was able to buy my original Geyer horn back. It had survived two other owners, and strangely enough I could make smooth slurs on it now. I don't know whether the horn got better or I did.

Geyer was a hands-on sort of guy. One time, Joe Egger was playing a concerto with the Grant Park Orchestra, so Carl Geyer, Farkas, Brouk, and I went to hear him. Afterward we all went to dinner. I remember Geyer telling Joe Egger, "You sound like a baritone horn. Come up to my shop, I will make you a mouthpiece."

In the 1950s and '60s, only large companies representing major brands were making horns. Now there are many private horn makers all over the world turning out a few horns each year. One of these is Karl Hill, who was a student of mine in Detroit. I played one of his horns, the Kortesmaki, for many years. I consider him to be a genius at or above the level of Carl Geyer.

The horn I ended up playing the most, especially for solos and concertos, was a Paxman Silver Descant that I bought from Neil Saunders in the '60s. Neil was an Englishman who had played second horn to Dennis Brain in the Philharmonia Orchestra and was teaching at Western Michigan University.

I sold both of these beautiful horns, the Geyer and the Paxman, to favorite students who are now using them in the Bay Area.

I owned two more great horns I should mention. The first was an older Conn 8D that I bought at my favorite Marin flea market for $200. I used that horn quite a bit for a year. The story about the $200 Conn 8D got around, and I got a call from an old gentleman who played in the San Francisco Golden Gate Park Band. He said his horn had been stolen a year before and he wondered if the horn I had found at the flea market was his. Turned out it was, and I had to give it back to him. He was very happy.

Another time I was having some work done on my horn at Dick Akright's shop in Oakland and went looking around in the back at the old junk horns. I found an old single B-flat horn that turned out to be a Geyer. I brought it out and asked Dick about it. He said, "That old thing? It's a piece of junk. It plays really out of tune."

It turned out that the horn's thumb valve was set up to stand in F, but the valve slides were of B-flat length. Using the thumb valve would put the horn into B-flat, and it would play fine. Obviously, anyone trying to play that horn standing in F with the B-flat slides would think it was out of tune.

We switched the thumb valve so the horn would stand in B-flat and it turned out to be a wonderful instrument. The number 23 was stamped on it which might have meant it was Geyer's 23rd horn. I sold that horn to Karl Hill, who completely reworked it with a new bell and lead pipe, which really improved an already great instrument.

Natural Horn

The natural horn is a predecessor of the French horn. It has no valves, but consists of a mouthpiece, long coiled tubing, and extra pieces of tubing used to change the length and thus the key. The natural horn was limited to playing only in the key associated with a particular length of tubing.

In order to play notes other than those on the natural harmonic series, you had to use your hand in the bell to alter the pitches. Playing chromatically on the natural horn by the use of the hand creates variations in the tone quality as well as the pitch.

The horn parts in early music up into the 19th century were written for natural horn in the key of the piece. The player chose the appropriate length of tubing to create a harmonic series in that key so that he could play most of the notes without having to alter the pitch by changing the position of his right hand in the bell.

Valves were invented in the early 19th century, coming into universal use by the beginning of the 20th century. With valves, modern horn players had a choice of 12 (or more) different lengths of tubing, each length with its own corresponding harmonic series, and an instrument which, if uncoiled, would stretch anywhere from nine to eighteen feet in length.

The valves make it possible to play chromatically without using the hand in the bell to change the pitch. When we play older music written for the natural horn, we use the valves to achieve the different keys and simply transpose mentally up or down.

Initially there was a lot of resistance to the new horns with valves that could play chromatically without changing the color of the sound. Composers such as Brahms continued to write for the natural horn even after valves were invented because they loved the sound.

Mozart wrote all his concertos for natural horn. Today, a few wonderful players such as Lowell Greer can play them on natural horn as originally intended, but it takes a special talent and a lot of years to learn how to do it well. Playing a piece on the natural horn produces a wonderful color palette since changing the pitch with the hand changes the color of the sound as well.

The Mozart concertos become a whole new experience for both performer and listener when played on natural horn. I once performed the Mozart Horn Concerto No. 1 on natural horn, but I never spent enough time on the other concertos that I was good enough to perform them.

Geyer made a natural horn for me that I used for the Britten Serenade. I still have it and even play it now and then. I had already fallen in love with the natural horn years before Geyer made that horn for me.

I found some recordings of tunes on the natural horn recorded by players from the Vienna Horn Club. I used them to demonstrate natural horns in masterclasses or workshops.

One time the San Francisco Symphony Orchestra went on tour to Vienna, and after the concert, several of us went out to have a beer with the players from the Vienna Philharmonic. I told them I had always loved hearing their recordings played on natural horns. Since they had their regular horns with them from the concert, they got them out and began to play hunting tunes. I knew the tunes, so I played along with them, even leading a little. They were shocked that this American guy knew these natural horn tunes. It was a great moment.

Alphorn

Once when I was skiing at Sugar Bowl with my wonderful ski partner and second horn Lori Westin, we heard an alphorn from the top of the mountain. I knew a little about alphorns because of my Swiss heritage, but I'd never owned one or even played one. We skied down and found an older gentleman on a platform in front of the restaurant area playing his alphorn. He was no expert, but he was doing okay. After he finished, he asked the people standing around listening, "Does anyone else want to try this?"

"Sure," I said, "I'll try it." The alphorn is a lot like the French horn. It's basically a natural horn made of wood. So I knew exactly what to do by instinct. I stomped up onto the platform like the ski bum I was, took the alphorn and played a Rossini piece that I had learned to play on the natural horn. It goes up and down and all over the place. It's quite a technical challenge, but it worked just great on the alphorn.

When I finished the piece I said to Lori, "Lori, this is fun! It's so easy, too. Want to try it?" She took the horn and played. The old alphorn player gaped at us with an obvious *What the hell?* expression. He seemed much relieved when we told him who we were and what we did for a living.

After that I had to have my own alphorn. My friend Bob Ward and I bought a matched pair pitched in F at the factory when we were on tour in Switzerland. We used them to play "Silent Night" on our Christmas record with the Bay Brass at Grace Cathedral.

Alphorn = free skiing

I started taking my alphorn with me when I went skiing. I hardly ever had to buy a lift pass after that. I would go to the office, give them a brief résumé, and tell them I'd play the alphorn at noon if they'd give me a free lift pass. It always worked.

When I retired, one of the directors on the symphony board who was also on the board of directors at Sugar Bowl gave me a certificate stating that I was the official alphorn player for Sugar Bowl.

Horn player Frank Lloyd had a carbon fiber alphorn that would collapse to a length of about 18 inches. You could really impress people by holding the big end and flicking it open like one of those folding cups you use for backpacking. It would zoom open to about 12 feet, a spectacular show. Plus, as it was only 18 inches long when collapsed, you could take it anywhere. I got one too and used it a lot when I taught at the Barry Tuckwell Institute in Colorado. Everyone got to play it. It was the only alphorn there.

Bob Ward, by the way, was a wonderful friend. Not only did we share a matched set of alphorns, but we often shared principal duties in the San Francisco Symphony until I left and he became principal.

Unlike me, Bob was capable of sight-reading anything. I only recently discovered that the reading problem I'd struggled with all my life had a name — dyslexia. In the orchestra, Bob and I were a matched pair in that I made him play the technically difficult twentieth century music (we called it "squeak-fart" music) while I relished performing the music of the 18th and 19th centuries.

PART V

❧

EDO DE WAART
(1975-1985)

—— 33. Too Old for This ——

Edo de Waart was a young Dutch conductor who had been an oboe player before going over to the dark side. He came to San Francisco in 1975 after Seiji Ozawa left for the Boston Symphony Orchestra. Because he was six or seven years younger than I, I felt that I could relate to him as an equal more than I could with the older conductors.

Maestro de Waart was the first boss that I could consider a friend. Except for Fiedler, no conductor I'd worked for had to endure more of my practical jokes or torment than Edo. For the most part, I think he was okay with that.

When he first got to San Francisco, Edo called me into his dressing room and told me that he liked young people in his orchestra. "How old are you?" he asked me.

"I don't have to tell you that," I said.

"Well, no, you don't have to tell me but I can look it up in your record and find out."

So I said, "Okay, okay! Thirty-six."

He said, "Thirty-six. Wow! That's great. You're about the same age as I am."

I said, "No. *Born* in thirty-six!"

He hemmed and hawed and said, "Well, okay, you look young, maybe you'll be alright."

It was easy to joust verbally with Edo. As I related earlier, in Bruckner's Symphony No. 4 there's a little passage in the last movement that jumps back and forth over about an octave and a half very lightly. I had forgotten about this passage as we blasted away on the heavy section that comes before. The horns were having a great time, pumping out the volume, playing those massive chords of Bruckner's for all they were worth, but this left me unprepared for the delicate little solo coming up. When I tried to play the solo, it didn't work at all. Thank God this was a rehearsal!

Edo stopped everything. "No, no, no! It goes like this," he said, and then sang it, a major "fagoto" (firm grasp of the obvious) on his part.

I said to him, "I know! It's easy to sing. I can sing it, too!" He glared at me and opened his mouth, but stopped short of saying anything. He just stepped back onto the podium and restarted the last movement.

A couple of weeks later I asked him how long it was going to take him to forgive me for that little remark. He said, "Oh, maybe another year or so."

Battle Between Just and Tempered Intonation

Just as Arthur Fiedler had done years before, Edo de Waart sometimes tried to tell the brass section to play *tempered* thirds when we always played *just* thirds. Usually we'd ignore him, but one time when we were rehearsing the Dvořák Serenade, we got to one of these places and he stopped us. "No!" He said, "You're out of tune."

"No, we're not," we said.

"Yes, you are!" he argued.

We just happened to have three electronic tuners on the stage. You can dial these tuners to produce any pitch desired. We tuned one of them to a C and another to a G. The third tuner we tuned to an E according to *just* intonation, which meant that we got this wonderful, resonant sound.

We said, "How do you like this?"

He said, "Give me the tuner." He turned the dial to tune the E a little sharper. We tried turning it back down again, asking him if he didn't like it better with the lower third, but no, he liked his high third better.

Finally we gave up. We realized he was just never going to hear it our way. He would always be trying to tell us we were out of tune, and we were always going to play in *just* intonation, never *tempered*. That's when we realized we were not put on this earth to teach conductors. Or religious leaders.

Just and Tempered Intonation

For those of you who are not horn players and may be wondering what the heck all this discussion about "natural harmonic series" and "just intonation" means, see Appendix D.

I must make a disclaimer about the use of *just* intonation. Since we horn players are so deeply involved with the harmonic series and use of the natural horn in classical music, we are especially aware of tuning when it involves major triads. The third in those triads must be *just* and not *tempered*. We don't worry about *just* intonation when we're playing the type of modern music that doesn't involve major triads.

〜♘

—— 34. SHENANIGANS IN —— SYMPHONY HALL

The Edo era was packed with banter between Edo and the orchestra members. We played lots of practical jokes to let off steam from the constant tension of performances. Also, as I've mentioned, I'd always had trouble with authority, and practical jokes helped me deal with authority figures like conductors.

Maybe some of these pranks went a little too far. When I tell people about some of my pranks (and those of other orchestra members), they look at me incredulously; after all, classical music is … what? Sacred? And those who perform it a little more dignified? But I've always enjoyed using humor to ease the intensity of this career I had chosen.

Sweater Vests

Here's an example of one prank I played on Edo that flopped, even though I had put a lot of effort into it, and some expense, too. Edo always wore sweater vests to rehearsals, so I went around to the different thrift stores I knew about and bought a bunch of sweater vests to pass out to the orchestra members.

When Edo came to rehearsal that day, there we were, all of us sitting in our chairs waiting to begin, wearing our sweater vests. He didn't notice at first. Then when he realized what we had done he got a little red in the face, but refused to comment, which was a disappointment to us pranksters. He also kept wearing sweater vests to rehearsals.

Chord/Beep — Beethoven 5th

Sometimes, the universe would play a prank back at me, usually in Edo's favor. In September 1980, the San Francisco Symphony moved to the newly constructed Louise M. Davies Symphony Hall across the street from the Opera House. This was cause for great celebration, since for the first time, the Symphony became completely separated from the Opera and the Opera House. We finally had our own home.

We held our opening concert on Sunday afternoon, September 14th. The San Francisco Symphony was televised live across the country playing Beethoven's Fifth Symphony with Maestro Edo de Waart conducting.

In the symphony's last movement is a passage where a chord sounds followed by a rest, the pattern repeating three times — chord/rest, chord/rest, chord/rest, chord/rest — followed by a tricky phrase for the horn in the lower register.

When we got to the passage in the concert, a loud beep sounded during the rest following the first chord. After each repetition of the chord, the same beep sounded again: chord/beep, chord/beep, chord/beep, chord/beep. After around the second iteration of this pattern, I realized what was happening. My watch alarm had gone off and, incredibly, was sounding a beep exactly on the rests between each chord.

I got badly flustered and was still hitting my wrist trying to silence the alarm when it came time to play my little solo passage.

Well, I jammed the horn up into my face and the passage came out terrible. It didn't work at all.

Later, I figured out that I only thought I had set my watch alarm for 4 a.m. Monday morning when we planned to wake up to go skiing. Instead, I'd set it 12 hours off so it went off at 4 p.m. during the concert.

The reviewers had it that some doctor's beeper had gone off and startled the horn player so that he completely messed up the passage.

For a while after that, when Edo would come onstage for a concert, he'd catch my eye, hold up his wrist, and look back and forth from me to his watch.

Trick or Treat

Once upon a Halloween, an audience was invited to attend our open rehearsal, and I wanted to do something special for the occasion. I was able to find a Hazmat suit and a gas mask. I had a hardhat, gloves, and some rubber boots. So I suited up, and when the orchestra was ready to tune, I walked out onto the stage in my costume, acting like I had been called in to investigate an environmentally challenged area. I had a meter with me, and as I walked through the violin section, I poked my meter around, looking under chairs.

The players didn't know who I was because of the gas mask, and everyone around me began to look like they were afraid something terrible had happened, or was about to happen, on stage.

Just at the point people seemed to be preparing for a quick exit, I stopped and took my seat in the horn section. Ahh, yes, it's Dave.

Glenn Fischthal

Besides me, we had several other comedians who kept the orchestra entertained during work. Glenn Fischthal was one.

We were on tour playing Mahler's 5th Symphony at Carnegie Hall. Our principal trumpet player, Glenn Fischthal, and the second trumpet player, Chris Bogios, loved to sit and talk together during rehearsals.

But on this occasion, we were waiting onstage after tuning for the concert. Edo de Waart came out, and the audience clapped. Edo turned to start the piece, and we all waited for Glenn's solo opening trumpet call. However, Glenn and Chris behind me were head to head in deep conversation.

I turned around and whispered urgently "Glenn, Glenn!" He raised his head and said, "Oh, yeah, just a minute." He made the audience, the orchestra, and the conductor wait while he finished what he was saying to Chris. When he was through he nodded to Edo, and we started the music.

Halloween Teeth

Another time we played Mahler's 5th on Halloween at Rutgers University in New Jersey. At the end of the piece, the audience applauded and I took my bow for the obbligato horn solo in the third movement.

When Glenn stood to take his bow for the opening trumpet solo, the audience and orchestra started laughing. I turned to see why they were laughing and saw Glenn grinning at the audience through a huge set of monster teeth he'd stuck in his mouth for Halloween.

Monster Piece

Glenn was notorious for being unprepared, always figuring he would learn on the job. Edo was conducting the first rehearsal of a modern piece that no one knew and that no one had ever played. Since this was a really modern piece and no one had heard it, who could tell if we were playing the right notes anyway?

The piece started with the orchestra making a lot of noise for about half a minute, and then everything stopped for a trumpet solo. I think Glenn was in the wrong key, maybe playing on a C trumpet when the part was in D, and he was having to transpose. The solo came out terribly — it was a total wreck. The whole orchestra froze and everything stopped. Edo said, "Mr. Fischthal, what seems to be the problem?"

Glenn said, "I don't know! I looked all over and I couldn't find the record anywhere!"

His comment completely defused a tense situation and the conductor said, "Well, okay, we'll try it again at the next rehearsal."

Edo's Sopranos

Throughout the orchestra, Edo was noted for his many wives, most of whom were sopranos. One time back when we were still with the opera, we were playing Beethoven's Fidelio. The opera includes a famous trio for the horn section. We loved to play that trio, and on this occasion we were really playing the heck out of it. It was so much fun!

I looked up from the orchestra and saw this gorgeous soprano on the stage. She saw me at about the same time, and we ogled each other for a while. A friend of mine nearby noticed and made a comment about it. I said, "Well, she likes our trio. And she's looking at me!"

"Careful, there," my friend said. "That's Edo's wife!"

"Oops!"

Sued!

In the early 1990's, my friend Bob Ward and I got the idea that we would play a joke on Edo, who had by this time left his tenure as our conductor to become music director of the Minnesota Orchestra. He had come back to San Francisco as a guest conductor.

Bob was really good with the computer and made a fake newspaper headline for the Minnesota *Times*. The headline read, "Noted Conductor Sued In Class Action Suit by Former Wives." In this suit, the fake article said, the former wives had found out that Edo had never been legally divorced from his first wife. We inserted this article into his score before the rehearsal.

When he came onstage for the rehearsal, Edo opened up his score to see this headline in the Minnesota newspaper about the lawsuit by his former wives. We watched him read it. Poor guy! He couldn't say or do anything. He had to conduct the first part of that rehearsal thinking that he was being sued by his former wives.

Of course, at the bottom of the article, we had written "Compliments of Bob and Dave," but he didn't have time to read that at first. I suppose that as soon as he figured out it was a joke, he would have known who had done it anyway.

Hello, Dolly

Even my sister Julie got in on some of the camaraderie. Julie is an accomplished artist. She can create anything with her painting, or sculpting, or a variety of other media. Once she made a pair of life-sized dolls that looked real. We called them the Hoschenpfeiffers. The old man had a porkpie hat and the old lady wore a grandma dress and thick-heeled black grandma shoes. They were a cute old couple. The minute I laid eyes on them I knew I had to take them to work with me.

My first prank was to seat them half-way back in the empty, dimly lit concert hall before rehearsal. People milling about onstage peered into the auditorium trying to figure out who the old couple was, sitting alone so quietly in the dark.

Next, I watched for my chance, then carried them into Maestro Edo's dressing room. I told him that my parents had come to visit and wanted to meet him and that they were waiting in his dressing room.

After another concert I carried them down to the music library and arranged them in the missionary position on a big flat table. They remained there overnight and totally freaked out the librarians the next morning when they unlocked the door to come in to work.

Mahler Cowbells

Some Mahler symphonies, including Mahler's Symphony No. 7, call for cowbells backstage. I was able to borrow someone's life-size, black and white plywood cow. During rehearsal, when they started ringing the cowbells in the second movement, I found a way to prop up this life-size cow behind the percussion section.

Everyone facing the percussion side of the stage started laughing. The violinists and all the other players who were facing the other direction wondered why everyone else was laughing — except for Edo, of course. He wasn't wondering *or* laughing.

Poor Bruce

In the late 1980s, the orchestra hired a new third horn, Bruce Roberts. All new hires had a probationary period of a year or so. If they survived it, they made tenure and became permanent members of the orchestra. But during that probationary period, they were employed only on a trial basis.

So we decided to play a trick on Bruce. We wrote a letter on Symphony stationery that said something like this: *We have been very happy with your playing so far, but there have been a few questions. For example, the time you forgot to bring your horn to rehearsal! We know you played in Mexico previously, and we're very worried about drugs, so we are granting you tenure on the condition that you have a pee test once a week for the next year.*

Poor Bruce, he read this letter while we all watched. He couldn't believe that the manager had really asked him to pee into a bottle! He finally figured out it was just a joke.

The Scent of Listerine

Years ago I found out that sanitizing my horn really helped my playing. I used Listerine. I'd pour a little of it into the mouthpiece and down into the lead pipe, shake it around a little bit, and dump it out. It just seemed to make the horn respond much better. The nearest I can figure out is that the alcohol in Listerine dissolved all the bubbly moisture inside the tubes. Furthermore, it seemed like the sanitary thing to do because who knows what ended up in there by the end of the day.

The only drawback was that the trumpet players sitting behind me always griped about it. They found the scent of Listerine blown from my horn back into their faces to be quite offensive.

Then one day I got a long letter in my mailbox from the lawyer of a drug company, explaining that he was the legal representative for the manufacturers of Listerine. They were covering their butts, saying that they disavowed any responsibility whatsoever for damage that might be done to the horn, either in the past or in the future, by my use of their product (Listerine) to clean it. I couldn't figure out why I had gotten this letter or how the company knew that I used Listerine on my horn.

It turned out that my friends in the orchestra had sent a letter to the company on my behalf, telling them how I used Listerine on my instrument. So Listerine had responded by having their lawyer reply with an official denial of any responsibility. You'd think they'd be happy I was using their product and would want to use me for an advertisement!

Your Uncles Play the Accordion!

My friend Mark Lawrence, who played principal in the trombone section behind me, had a friend, Barbara Butler, who was a very good trumpet player. She and her husband Charles Geyer were both trumpet professors at Northwestern University. They played together a lot. The trumpet world wasn't very kind to women at that time, so Barbara was on her own, unique as a female trumpet player.

Barbara didn't know me at all. Mark and I were roommates on tour in New York for a concert at Carnegie Hall. We were sitting in our hotel room when we got the idea of calling up Barbara. Mark and Barbara had been playing practical jokes on each other for years.

I developed this idea that I would pose as the personnel manager of the Detroit Symphony and offer her a week of employment subbing as principal trumpet. So I called her up and pretended to be the personnel manager. I told her our first trumpet player had a minor accident and wouldn't be able to play at all the next week. We needed a substitute to come in and play principal trumpet.

"Your name came up," I told her. "The program is Scriabin's *Poem of Ecstasy,* and, as you know, there is a big trumpet solo, so we want to know some of your qualifications." I got her into talking about her career all the way back to high school, when she won solo contests.

She was so eager to get this assignment! I just kept listening and saying, "Uh-huh. Is there anything more?" Finally, I said, "Well, Barbara, what we really want to know is, can you play like a man?"

She said, "I don't know who the f--- you are, but you've got to be a friend of Mark Lawrence's." She knew she'd been had! And I was so embarrassed getting her to tell me every solo she had ever played.

Once she met me and found out who I was, it became her mission to retaliate and she did so quite skillfully.

Soon after we played our trick on Barbara, we played a concert in San Francisco at Davies Hall. After the concert the players were milling around backstage and a woman came in who introduced herself as a reporter from CBS who was looking for somebody to interview. I happened to be standing right near her, so I asked if I could help her.

She said, "Well, there is a proposition in front of the Board of

Supervisors to make the accordion the official instrument of San Francisco. We'd like some comments."

I said, "I'd be glad to comment."

So we went out onstage. The audience was gone by now, and I was the only one left in the hall along with the interviewer and the cameraman. She asked again what I thought of the accordion becoming the official instrument of San Francisco.

I said, "Well, you know, for one thing, the definition of a gentleman is somebody who knows how to play the accordion but chooses not to. And, if this proclamation happens, we are going to print up bumper stickers that say *Use an Accordion, Go To Jail!*" When my mother heard about the interview, she said, "Why, your uncles play the accordion!"

I figured that was the end of that, but it went on National news. Barbara heard about it and couldn't let it alone. A couple of weeks after the news story broke, I got a call from a guy with this rather mafioso voice who said he was from the Accordion Anti-Defamation League in Wisconsin and they were putting a price on my head. I was no longer allowed to enter the state of Wisconsin. Barbara had hired an actor to pull this off.

Paging ...

Our shenanigans around the world didn't end in symphony halls, nor did we waste time idling around in airports. When we'd go on tour with SFO, we spent a lot of time in airports, and my friends and I would take advantage of the paging systems there. We enjoyed having weird people paged, like obscure conductors or composers and sometimes even well-known people.

At that time Ernest Fleischmann was CEO of the Los Angeles Philharmonic, and our executive director was Peter Pastreich. We often felt that those two were in competition — a San Francisco vs. Los Angeles thing.

I always got the impression Peter Pastreich felt a little intimidated by Ernest Fleischmann. Ernest always had grand designs. I fantasized that he would come up to San Francisco and take over, and the San Francisco Symphony and Los Angeles Philharmonic would become one giant California organization rather than two separate orchestras. Fleischmann was very powerful.

Sometimes when we were at an airport with our executive director Peter Pastreich and had a clear view of his face, we'd have Ernest Fleischmann paged and then watch Peter tense up as his eyes darted around, looking for Fleischmann.

Pastreich and Liberace

Speaking of Peter Pastreich, I never realized he had a sense of humor until I found out that when Liberace died, Pastreich made up a concert program in tribute to Liberace as a great musician and artist. He had four or five copies of the program printed up and put them in the audience box at Davies Hall where the Board of Directors sat.

The Board of Directors came to the concert, picked up their programs, and saw that the San Francisco Symphony evidently had paid tribute to Liberace by devoting an entire program to him. They were really pissed. They went running up to Pastreich, saying, "How could you do this?" not realizing that they had the only four copies of the Liberace-themed programs. All the rest of the programs in the hall were the regular ones. So he'd pulled a fast one on them.

Skiing in Tails

Mark Lawrence and I liked to ski together. One time I got the idea to ski in our full concert tailcoat outfits just to shake everyone up. So we dressed up in our full dress tails and skied in them. I'm sure we looked ridiculous! When people asked us why we were dressed like that, I said, "My friend Mark here is getting married at the top of Lift Three at 1:00 this afternoon, and you're all invited. I'm the preacher."

At 1:00 Mark and I stood at the bottom of the lift looking up and watching while a group of people gathered at the top of Lift Three waiting for a wedding to happen. Of course it didn't happen. Later on while we were still skiing people kept coming up to us asking, "What happened to the wedding?"

I told them, "Well, the bride got cold feet!"

Full Dress: Mark Lawrence and David Krehbiel

Not Afraid of Tyrants

I'd finally gotten over my fear of tyrant conductors, so George Cleve of San Jose didn't bother me much. But I can't speak for the members of his orchestra, the San Jose Symphony.

When the famous horn player Hermann Baumann cancelled at the last minute before a concert, I was invited to take his place, and I played two concertos, Mozart's Horn Concerto No. 4 and Strauss's Horn Concerto No. 1, on the same program with Cleve in San Jose. I was amazed at how he stomped around belligerently through his orchestra, belittling them and talking down to them. I heard nothing encouraging or positive from him.

Cleve may have been a tyrant with his own orchestra but not when he guest-conducted ours. Anytime he guest-conducted us in San Francisco, he was Mr. Nice Guy, and it always seemed like he was trying to ingratiate himself to us somehow.

One of the times Cleve guest-conducted, Mark and I were coming around the corner heading toward the stage entrance at Davies Hall. George Cleve pulled up in an antique limousine and stepped out. As Mark and I watched, he greeted us with a wave, a "Hi guys!" and a big, flashy smile, and planted his foot in a huge pile of dog shit. Squish! That must have been embarrassing enough, but now he had to conduct a rehearsal standing at the podium of this orchestra he was trying to impress, his shoe reeking.

Just desserts for tyrant conductors!

On the topic of dog shit, one time Floyd Cooley, our tuba player, set his tuba down in a pile of it outside before a concert and didn't notice. You know how the tuba sits in the tuba player's lap. Soon the stuff was smeared all over his pants and tailcoat. Talk about embarrassing!

〜

————— 35. FUN WITH BRASS —————

As I have mentioned before, I've always loved playing in and conducting different kinds of brass groups, mostly large groups of 12-14 people, usually during symphony orchestra off-seasons.

Bay Brass at Grace

My friends in San Francisco started a group called Bay Brass, made up from some of the best brass players from the area's opera, ballet, and symphony orchestras. There were four trumpets, four horns, four trombones, a tuba, and percussion. I became the conductor.

Many of our concerts were unique. We played Christmas concerts in San Francisco's Grace Cathedral, and made a recording of our Christmas tunes there.

One year I got the idea of playing "We Three Kings" on Wagner tubas. We called it "Entrance of the Wise Tubas." We dressed up three of our horn players in robes. I got an idea that the Wise Tubas should also bear a gift. A friend from church happened to be at the concert with her angelic-looking young son of about eight, and I enlisted him in our efforts. I wrapped my collapsed carbon fiber alphorn in gold paper and placed it on a big velvet pillow I'd found.

Our three horn players, dressed in robes, walked from the back of the cathedral down the central aisle to the front, playing "We Three Kings" on the Wagner tubas. The angelic child followed them, holding the velvet pillow with my wrapped alphorn lying on top. It was great theater.

When the three wise tubas reached me at the front of the cathedral they presented me with the gift, and I unwrapped it. Now, a collapsed carbon fiber alphorn is about 18 inches long until you open it up, which you do by shaking it. When shaken, it zooms out to 12 feet. As I've noted, it's quite spectacular to see the horn fly open like that.

I then played "Amazing Grace," which fits well with the notes available on the alphorn. It seemed appropriate as well to play "Amazing Grace" in Grace Cathedral.

Another idea I had for a Grace Cathedral concert was to play Christmas carols on conch shells. I enlisted everyone to bring their best conch shells to a rehearsal where we found out who could play what note, and on which conch shell. There were eight of us, each of us with a conch shell that played a certain note. We played the notes in sequence to create the tune of a Christmas carol. We were like those trained seals you see sometimes, each of them blowing a horn.

In the middle of the concert I made a mistake and played at the wrong time. We all started to laugh, but somehow we stumbled through playing the rest of the Christmas carol on our conch shells.

I thought it would be fun to do something with Grace Cathedral's incredible acoustics, which created a seven-second reverb. I devised an idea of distributing the brass choir players around the perimeter of the cathedral, 20 to 30 feet apart. We played what I called the "Grace Amen."

Starting at one end of the cathedral, a group of players would make a staggered entrance on the notes of the subdominant chord (the "A" in "Amen"), each player holding his note for a specific duration. As these players each released their notes, the adjacent group of players would come in on the same staggered entrance, and so on down the line.

In this way, the audience would hear the "A" in "Amen" travel all the way around the inside of the cathedral in a kind of continuous rolling surround-sound wave. After the wave worked its way around the church, there'd be a brief pause, and then the same process would repeat on the tonic chord (the "men" in "Amen").

The organ at Grace Cathedral is huge. The console is portable and can be moved around the apse. When Bay Brass first started playing at the church, the umbilical cord full of wires from the organ to the pipes was about six inches in diameter. Later, they modernized it and now it's a sleek fiber-optic cable. It's only about three-quarters of an inch in diameter but it still manages to hook up thousands and thousands of pipes and everything else it takes to run the organ.

At first, John Fenstermaker, the church organist and choirmaster for Grace Cathedral played the organ for us at our concerts, but he moved to Florida. The church hired an organist to take his place, a young woman who was new and a little green.

During one of our tunes, "Oh Come All Ye Faithful," the brass group stops in the middle, and out of the silence the organ comes in full blast. However, at the concert when the brass came to that point and stopped, the organ did not play. One, two, three, four seconds passed in a shocked silence.

I watched the organist frantically struggle at the stops and switches of the organ, seemingly trying to figure something out. Finally the organ came blasting in and we continued the song.

As it turned out, the organ had a kill switch used to silence the organ temporarily. When sliding on and off the organ bench it is easy to hit a pedal with your foot or hit a key with your hands and make an inadvertent noise. The organist had engaged the kill switch and totally forgotten she had done so.

Summit Brass

Mark Lawrence and I attended an all-brass symposium at Indiana University where we saw a lot of our friends. On the bus back to the airport we ran into David Hickman, who was a trumpet soloist and professor at Arizona State University. He told us he was thinking about forming a brass group that would be made up of the best players from orchestras all around the country, and he wanted our recommendations. We recommended Gail Williams (horn), Joe Alessi (trombone), and Tony Plog (trumpet) as well as two trumpet players from New York.

At the time, Mark and I thought, *well this guy is a dreamer and the idea will probably never materialize.* But, sure enough, it came together. We called it Summit Brass, and it's still going. I was a member from the time it started in 1985 and conducted it for several years. I retired from Summit Brass quite a few years ago.

Every year Summit Brass held a one-week summer camp, usually in Colorado at Keystone Resort in Summit County (hence the group's name). Some of the players would drive all the way out from New York to play for a week at this camp.

One year, the principal trombone player from New York Philharmonic, Joe Alessi, was with the New York group driving to Keystone.

They stopped at a turnout overlooking a scenic view into a canyon. Joe just couldn't stand it — he had to go get his trombone and play out over the canyon. Quite a few tourists had also stopped at the popular turnout and were awed as they listened to the sound of the trombone reverberating through the canyon.

One of the tourists came up to him afterward and said, "Wow! That sounded fantastic. You ought to be in the New York Philharmonic."

Joe laughed. "Well, I am!" he said.

We had a lot of fun with alphorns in Summit Brass. Gail Williams, formerly with the Chicago Symphony Orchestra, and now a teacher at Northwestern and a friend of mine, had a carbon fiber alphorn like mine. We would take these horns on tours with Summit Brass.

I had the idea to go out on stage at a Summit Brass concert, flip open my collapsible alphorn (which, as related, was very exciting in itself) and then give a brief lecture about it. I would explain what the alphorn was, how long it was, and fascinate the audience with stories about the magical sounds the Swiss locals made with their horns that echoed across the valleys of Switzerland and the Alps.

Then as I demonstrated the sound of my alphorn, Gail would echo the same sound from her instrument backstage. At first, the audience usually believed that the sound of her horn was an authentic echo of my own. I'd play a little bit more and Gail would echo again.

Then I'd play a little more, but her response would be just a little different from mine. Then the next time, she would improvise a little bit. Then I'd play and Gail would answer with a completely different melody from backstage, and people finally got it.

I had quite an embarrassing moment on one of our Summit Brass tours. On our winter tours, we'd fly into a larger city and from there each day we'd climb on a bus to play one night stands in surrounding cities. On one particular tour we'd flown into St. Louis. The conductor traveling with us was Henry David Smith, assistant conductor of the Philadelphia Orchestra and a former trombone player. He was a dignified, lovable old gentleman.

We'd spend most of our daytimes on the bus. By mid-day, the bus was often quite rowdy. We'd party, joke around, and play poker. On this occasion, when it got to be joke time, I decided to tell a joke to Allen Dean and Ray Mase, two trumpet players from New York.

Now the joke was anti-fundamentalist religion, and very long, and was ultimately a terrible joke. In the middle of telling this joke I noticed my audience had started laughing and I wondered, *Why are they laughing? I'm only part way through the joke!* But they continued laughing all the way through.

Later they told me that Smith had been sitting in the seat in front of them and had probably heard the joke. They informed me he was a religious fundamentalist. I'm sure he must have been offended by my terrible joke.

The trumpet players knew that and they didn't tell me. They just kept laughing and egging me on to complete the joke while Smith, very nice gentleman conductor that he was, never said a word.

LA Brass Quintet

The two young trumpet players I met at College of the Pacific music camp when we were kids, Mario Guarneri and Thomas Stevens, later became members of the Los Angeles Philharmonic Orchestra and the Los Angeles Brass Quintet. When the Quintet needed a substitute horn player for a while, they flew me down from San Francisco.

We received an invitation to play at a trumpet symposium being held in Boulder, Colorado. One of the featured artists at this symposium was Jean-Pierre Mathez, editor of the *Brass Bulletin*, a Swiss magazine well known in Europe to most trumpet players. The first night's concert featured Mathez.

The audience was made up of trumpet players wearing intent expressions and cluttering the aisles with their trumpet cases, some of which contained so many trumpets that they looked like suitcases. They were sitting and waiting for the European trumpet player Jean-Pierre to show them what a European trumpet player could do.

To help set up this story, let me tell you what one of my teachers at Northwestern once told me about the premiere performance in this country of Strauss's *Salome*, held at the Lyric Opera in Chicago. The impresario of the opera was Mary Garton. Evidently, there was an injunction against the performance of *Salome* for being too radical and anti-religious, and it had to go through the courts, but finally, after a lengthy court battle, Chicago Opera got permission to premiere *Salome*. It was a huge event.

Before the performance, Garton raised the temperature in the hall to about 90 degrees and bathed it in red light, and then she delayed the start of the performance for at least an hour.

Here was this audience sweltering in the heat, bathed in red light, and sitting in a hall waiting for the premiere to begin. On and on the delay went. People became furious, frustrated. Why is it so hot in here? Why are they stalling? But no one could leave because this was the big premiere! When the opera finally began, the impact on the audience was much greater as a result of this intense build-up. To set up an audience like this was a work of genius resulting in a most moving experience for them.

Well, we got to the evening performance of this trumpet player from Europe and sat waiting in the hall — all those trumpet players and me with the LA Brass Quintet. It didn't start. And it didn't start. We sat for half an hour and it still didn't start. No one could leave because we were all so anxious to see what this trumpet player from Europe could do. The stage was totally dark.

Finally after about 45 minutes, the lights came up a little bit, just barely enough to see. From the right hand corner of the stage emerged an ancient gray-haired man, bent with arthritis, who could barely move, holding his trumpet by the crook, the bell dragging on the floor. He stumbled and shuffled out onto the stage. The stage lit up to reveal a rug and a rocking chair. It took the old man a long time to shuffle out to his rocking chair and finally manage to plop down into it.

After taking some time to recover, he gradually moved the trumpet toward his lips and his lips moved ever so slowly toward the trumpet, like a bird trying to get a drink of water from a cup. When his lips finally touched the mouthpiece he began making some strange sounds, slobbering on the trumpet.

My friends and I were roaring with laughter, but the rest of the audience didn't understand that this was performance art. Trumpet players are a very serious group, and they were really pissed off.

The European trumpet player Mathez never once played a legitimate note on his trumpet during the symposium. He did a piece called "Water Music," where he came out, sat on his rocking chair, and placed a microphone in the bell of the trumpet. Then he took a glass of water and poured it into the trumpet. When he blew air into the trumpet it would gurgle and bubble and he would get a kind of rhythm going. I'm sure the trumpet world couldn't believe what was happening.

The next night, the members of the LA Brass Quintet were the featured artists. We all had trumpets. I had a bass trumpet. Miles, the trombone player, had a bass trumpet pointing forward, and Roger, the tuba player, had developed some sort of tuba, a big fat thing with a bell that pointed straight out at the audience.

I'd gotten the idea that we would mimic what Mathez did. We started with a totally dark stage, dragging ourselves on from the corners of the stage, imitating the way the old trumpet player had come out in the semi-darkness. When we finally got to the front of the stage and started to raise up our trumpets, the lights came full onto us and we played this brilliant piece, five trumpets, that was Bam!! right into their faces. It was spectacular!

LA Brass — Left to right: Miles Anderson, David Krehbiel, Mario Guarneri, Tom Stevens, Roger Bobo

I had to work hard to convince our trumpet player Tom to do this. He thought this would be a big insult to Mathez. I kept saying, "No! He's going to like it." Well he loved it! The audience loved it!

Carmel Bach Festival

I was often asked to play at various music festivals in the summers. One was the Carmel Bach Festival, where I had the thrilling experience of playing the horn solo in the *Quoniam* from Bach's B Minor Mass. I got to sing the Mass with the choir, and when it was time for the *Quoniam*, I stepped out with my horn and played. I've always thought of this solo as the voice of God, and I feel it must be played with that in mind.

Another of the memorable experiences in the Carmel Bach Festival was playing the Brandenburg Concerto No. 2, a very strenuous piece with a part usually played by the trumpet in an extremely high register. There has been talk over the years that it should be played an octave lower on something like the horn. This makes sense because if the part is played on the horn an octave lower, it doesn't completely dominate the other soloists. I played it on the horn an octave lower at Carmel. I had never done it before, and it was really fun. That was the only time I ever played it.

That performance was not without a memorable comedic moment. After the first movement, the oboe player, Ray, was sweating profusely and the audience was deadly quiet. Ray reached in his pocket to pull out a handkerchief. In the handkerchief were some coins which started sliding out of the handkerchief and clattering to the plywood floor of the temporary stage.

The audience tittered a little and then quieted down. Ray decided he couldn't continue playing with his handkerchief hanging half-way out of his pocket, so, not knowing what else to do, he pulled it out the rest of the way. All the rest of the coins clattered noisily to the floor. The audience lost it then. I don't think I've ever heard an audience laugh like that, but somehow we managed to finish the piece.

San Luis Obispo Mozart Festival

Another summer music festival in which I participated regularly was the Mozart festival in San Luis Obispo. Out of the orchestra, we formed a brass quintet, called the San Luis Obispo Mozart Festival Brass Quintet.

I met a wonderful trumpet player and composer, Tony Plog, who is now retired and had become a good friend of mine. Tony was also a member of the quintet. We would go up into the belfry of the mission in San Luis Obispo and serenade the city from there. The priest told us not to ring the bell. But, of course, we rang the bell all the time.

We had a good time with that brass quintet. In fact, the whole wind section of that orchestra was always very social, and we were all good friends. We decided to have a party. This was when hot tubs were first getting popular.

I found a nightclub up on a hill in San Luis Obispo that rented hot tubs, and we made arrangements to rent a large one, maybe 12 feet in diameter. All of us from the wind section drank beer and partied in the hot tub *sans* swimsuits, except for one trumpet player who brought swim goggles and swam around in the hot tub.

After our party in the hot tub, the members of the brass quintet thought it would be a great idea to go serenade the customers at the Spyglass Inn, so down we went with our instruments. The customers there were mostly older people dancing to Hawaiian music played on an electric organ and accompanied by a singer doing Hawaiian bird calls. The manager told us we could play as soon as the Hawaiian musicians were finished.

We got out our instruments and waited for the group to finish their bird calls. While we waited, Tony Plog got his trumpet out and began playing jazz licks based on the bird calls, which got us laughing uncontrollably.

The Hawaiian group finally finished and someone announced that we were the Mozart Festival Brass Quintet, and that we were going to play Die Bänkelsängerlieder. We started to play, but we lasted only maybe two measures before all hell broke loose because we were still laughing so hard we were leaking air from around the mouthpiece.

What a disaster. I was so embarrassed. "Come on, guys," I said. "We've got to try this again."

We tried again, and this time we lasted about four measures before we fell apart again. We stopped and tried the third time with the same result. After the fourth attempt, we finally gave up. It was apparent that we weren't going to be able to get through it. My wife, Carol, was there, too, feeling very humiliated.

So we packed up our instruments and walked out the door as the announcer said, "We'd like to thank the San Luis Obispo Mozart Brass Quintet for their lovely performance." I am sure our quintet holds the world's record for being unable to play a tune due to laughing. What we didn't realize at the time was that we had done our own version of performance art!

Excerpts for Horn

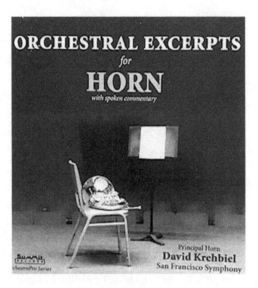

In 1993, five years before I retired, my friend David Hickman, who was then head of Summit Records, called me into his dressing room during a Summit Brass tour and told me they were thinking of making some CDs of the brass excerpts from the orchestral literature most commonly asked for at auditions. They wanted to know if I would like to record the horn excerpts.

I jumped at the chance. I loved those pieces so much and I loved those famous solos. No one had done this before, so I agreed to do it, thinking it would be easy. I thought I would go to the studio and play the excerpts, improvise a little, and talk about each one.

As I began to prepare for the recording session, I found I could play the excerpts just fine, but I got tongue-tied when I had to describe how I felt playing them. I had to write all my comments out and get them organized.

We recorded the CD in a church in Monrovia in Southern California. The recording engineer was Sonny Ausman, second trombone in the LA Philharmonic and an excellent recording engineer. Sonny had assured me that everything would be quiet, but we had to stop a number of times because a loud car or motorcycle sped by. Lori Weston, the second horn player from San Francisco Symphony, joined me for the excerpt from Bach's Brandenburg Concerto No. 1, which we played together.

This recording became very successful, the first of its kind. It set the stage for other artists to make similar audition excerpt CDs for the trumpet, the trombone, the tuba, the woodwinds, the English horn, and even the strings.

The story has it that after a certain take — one that I didn't think went very well — you can hear some swear words on the recording if you have the volume turned up really loud, although I've never been able to hear them.

So far we've sold five or six thousand of those CDs, and many young students have listened to it. Of course, the CD is rather obsolete now because with the Internet you can instantly access any excerpt or piece you want to listen to.

But it's interesting that even now, whenever I do a masterclass or when horn students meet me for the first time, they can't quite get over the sound of my voice in person being the same sound they've heard in their ears many times on the CD. Making that CD and getting to express my emotions about each one of those pieces was a wonderful experience.

— 36. MORE SHENANIGANS —

The Noisy Trombones

This is probably the most important story I have to tell, because out of all the things I ever did — all the concertos I played, all the solos I played on recordings, all the teaching I did — this is probably the deed for which I'll be most remembered in the world of orchestra players.

We were rehearsing Stravinsky's *The Fairy's Kiss,* which happens to be one of my favorite pieces. In the middle of the piece I stood up, turned around, and yelled at my friend Mark Lawrence in the trombone section, "The trombones are too damn loud! I can't *stand* it anymore! I'm gonna have to take action."

Mark said, "Okay, Dave, now just calm down. Calm down! Let's go backstage and we'll talk about it and we'll work it out."

I said, "No! I have to do something right now. I can't stand it." So I walked over to him, grabbed his trombone, and threw it down on the stage floor. I jumped and stomped on it ferociously. Then I stalked off the stage.

Some of the orchestra members knew it was a joke but many didn't. In fact the entire viola section started cheering because they'd always thought the trombones were too loud.

The prank was realistic because I was kind of nervous about it. My voice was shaky and sounded like it was full of emotion. I must have sounded as though I'd suddenly gone off the deep end.

Well, this was a big hit with the orchestra. The story spread all over the orchestra world. Everyone remembers it, even now.

The Sunday before this rehearsal, I had once again been to the flea market and found an old trombone for ten dollars. It was pretty funky-looking and I polished it up so it would look respectable.

I had arranged with Mark that as soon as I stood up and started harassing him he would quickly sneak his good trombone down to the side of his chair and pick up the ten-dollar trombone from the flea market. This was the one I grabbed and stomped on.

For a long time after that, when I'd meet people in the halls, string players especially, they would clutch their instruments protectively to their bodies. David Atherton, conductor of the San Diego Symphony, was the guest conductor that week. I had told him about the prank beforehand. I wasn't about to do something like that without the conductor knowing.

Another Horn Audition

Listening to auditions for a job in the orchestra is an emotionally exhausting task. We may hear more than sixty players, each with their own hopes and dreams of making a living by filling the one spot open in our horn section. That five minutes onstage is the culmination of years of study and practice.

After one long day of horn auditions, maybe about thirty of them, I came home, fixed myself a large drink, and settled in for some welcome relaxation. The phone rang. It was one of the auditioners, and he wanted me to give him my comments on his audition. I asked him where he was from. He said he was from St. Louis and had studied with Roland Pandolfi, principal horn of the St.

Louis Symphony. I asked him for his audition number and went to find my notes on each of the auditioners for that day.

When I found the comments corresponding to his audition number, I had to tell him that the reason he didn't advance to the finals was that he played very sharp to the piano, with no attempt to adjust his intonation.

He said, "I never play sharp!"

I told him that I was only trying to help, and that my notes said he played very sharp.

He said, "Your ears must be f---ed, because I never play sharp!"

The more I tried to calm him and help him understand the problem, the more confrontational he became.

After some time, I began to feel that there was something familiar about this voice yelling at me from a hotel room somewhere.

It turned out to be my best friend Mark Lawrence, who had also been at the audition. He had stuffed napkins in his mouth to disguise his voice, and was trying to see how long it would take to get me to hang up on him.

One of Mark's finest!

Mark's New Car

Mark bought a brand new Alfa Romeo sports car. He was very proud of it. I told our friends in the orchestra that we should go out after the concert to check it out.

Meantime, at intermission, I went out to the parking lot and jacked up one of the rear tires. After the concert, all of our friends came out to admire his new sports car.

Mark got in behind the wheel, and I got in on the passenger's side. He started the car, put it in gear, and nothing happened.

It didn't take long for Mark to figure out who did that. Gotcha, Mark!

Masterclass in Banff

We all got so used to our own banter onstage and off that sometimes it became difficult to tell what was real and what was not, whom to believe and whom not to believe.

I got a call from someone who wanted to pay me a lot of money to come to Banff for a masterclass. I knew this had to be another joke, so I said, "Is there any good skiing there?" This person said, "Yes, and if you come you can ski for a day or two."

This was way too good to be true, so I kept asking stupid questions about it. Well, after a while, it turned out to be for real, so I had to explain and apologize. I did have a great trip and got in some great skiing in Banff.

One of My Finest

Then there was the time I saved Diane Feinstein's ass.

The San Francisco Symphony was on tour in Washington DC and there was a reception for us in the Library of Congress. I found Senator Feinstein at the reception and told her straight out that I had saved her ass.

With a smile, she said, "Tell me how!"

I told her about how, years ago, when she was Mayor of San Francisco, the orchestra was set up outside at Union Square to celebrate giving the Key to the City to Willie McCovey. Somehow — and this was happening right at the back of the orchestra where I sat in the horn section — a couple of helium balloons had gotten caught on the back of her skirt and were slowly lifting it up. Without even thinking, I reached over and unhooked the balloons. No one ever knew. This really happened.

She laughed and told me that this had happened to her once before, when she was in charge of opening the rodeo exhibition at the Cow Palace in Daly City, California. A trick roper had circled her with his lasso. When he lifted the lasso up, it pulled her skirt up and exposed her.

One Hundred Pictures

After Edo de Waart left the orchestra, he came back as guest conductor many times. After all my time with him, I knew exactly what he'd do when he arrived for the first rehearsal. He'd come out onto the podium, mumble "Good morning," then put his head down and without looking at us would mention unconvincingly how great it was to be back with us.

I went down to the music library and ran off about 100 photocopies of what looked like a mug shot of Edo from a PR picture I had of his smiling face. Before rehearsal I passed the copies out to everyone in the orchestra and told them that when he lowered his head to talk down at the floor, they were to hold this picture up to their faces.

He came out onstage and sure enough, lowered his head to look at the floor as he told us how great it was to be there, and the participants from the orchestra held his picture up to their faces so that when he looked up he saw 90 people wearing his face. He looked straight at me. After all these years he knew who was responsible for that one.

With Edo de Waart

Well, now I had 100 copies of de Waart's smiling face, and I couldn't really let them go to waste, could I? The hallway through the stage-level dressing rooms of Davies Hall abounds with pictures of famous artists and conductors who have performed there. I scotch-taped the copies of de Waart's photos onto the faces of the artists in the pictures so that all the pictures in the hallway were of de Waart.

I sat down on a bench under the pictures waiting for him to come in for the day's rehearsal. When he arrived, he walked directly over to me and mumbled, "What have you got going on now? I know *something's* going on here!" I just grinned at him and pointed above my head. He looked up and saw that every photograph in the place had his face on it. Even Edo had to laugh.

*When my friends found out what I had done to Edo with the pictures,
they did the same thing to me at a faculty concert backstage at the
Lobero Theatre in Santa Barbara.*

PART VI

❧

THE BLOMSTEDT YEARS
(1985-1996)

37. HUMANNESS IN PERFORMANCE

Herbert Blomstedt was something new and different for me. At first I was rather put off by his seemingly awkward conducting. But by the end of his tenure with the orchestra, I was a true believer. The music he loved was the music I loved. Everything he did was heartfelt.

We recorded all the Nielsen and Sibelius symphonies with him. His Mahler was always wonderful. In a way, he was the opposite of Ozawa in that a Blomstedt recording always revealed a special humanness that took the music past mere technical perfection.

Performing without humanness is like being an actor in a play and learning your part in a foreign language, phonetically reciting the words, but having no idea what the words mean. How do you express a feeling if you don't understand what the words mean?

So many people play music like that, as though it's a language they can recite but they don't know the inflections or understand the meaning or the emotion behind each note and behind each phrase. Almost anyone can memorize the notes, but understanding the meaning and emotion behind those notes and communicating those qualities in a performance is a completely different level of playing.

When we speak, we inflect automatically out of our intent or our emotions. Our voice goes up and down, we accent and we phrase our voice, and we don't have to think about it consciously. It just happens.

Similarly, trying to communicate music by just thinking and knowing what the black marks on the page are doesn't work. Many students, even professional musicians, play music from the intellectual center. But what drives everything is emotion. There has to be emotion behind the thought. If there is a wall, if the thinking doesn't create an emotion, there's no humanness in the performance.

So it's crucial to free our thinking from physical actions and techniques, or black marks on a page, so that our minds can empower and connect with the emotions behind those marks.

Bruckner Horn Section with Wagner Tubas — Front (left to right): Jonathan Ring, Bruce Roberts, Eric Aiken, Bob Ward. Back (left to right): Doug Hull, Bill Klingelhoffer, Lori Westin, David Krehbiel, Chris Cooper

An Alpine Symphony

In my entire career, I'd never played Richard Strauss's tone poem *Eine Alpensinfonie* (*An Alpine Symphony*). Now, with Maestro Blomstedt in San Francisco, it had come up on the program, and I was excited. But I was also worried because I knew there was a lot of important hornplaying in it. So I bought a CD to become better acquainted with the piece.

Several days after I bought the CD, I decided to join my wife and kids who had driven down earlier to visit our farm in Reedley. I got up before dawn on a Sunday morning and began the 200 mile drive to the farm. There wasn't another car out at that hour as I sped south on the lonely stretch of Interstate 5 between Tracy and Los Banos. I remembered the CD of *Eine Alpensinfonie* I had with me and put it in the player.

As the music heralding daybreak and the light of the rising sun surrounded me, the eastern sky began to brighten. The sun's first sliver of light gradually illuminated the snow-capped Sierra, and then, like magic, daylight splayed itself across the sky just as Strauss's lavish sonic depiction of daybreak poured through the car's speakers.

It was an ethereal experience I'll never forget, and it would not have been the same had the orchestra played the symphony note-perfect without expressing the nuances of feeling behind the notes. Later, we were able to record the Alpine Symphony. I think I put a few extra notes in that one just for fun.

Cleveland and Tchaikovsky's Fourth

Not every conductor or musician interprets a piece the same.

When the Cleveland Orchestra came to San Francisco on tour, I got a last minute phone call to come and help out in their horn section because several of their members were absent. They needed me to assist the principal horn with Tchaikovsky's Fourth Symphony. So with no rehearsal, I went onstage at the concert to assist.

Tchaikovsky Four opens with a horn fanfare in octaves. In San Francisco Symphony, we always played that fanfare very connected and sustained. However, Cleveland played the fanfare detached with space between the notes. When we played the first note of the symphony, it turned out to be a one-note solo as I sustained it through the beat as we did in San Francisco, while Cleveland played it detached.

But I quickly realized that Cleveland had a different interpretation and switched with the next note to their more detached style. I found that I enjoyed the symphony played in a different style, and

I realized that their interpretation was as valid as mine.

Also, I got to add to my résumé that I had played with the Cleveland Orchestra.

A Little Morality Please!

Maestro Blomstedt had the conductor's dressing room completely redecorated when he came to San

Francisco. Edo, during his tenure with San Francisco Symphony, had decorated the room in a Southwestern, Georgia O'Keefe style. But Blomstedt had all of that removed, and he redecorated with antique Chippendale.

Maestro Blomstedt was noted to be religious, a devout Seventh Day Adventist. Not long after he started with San Francisco, he had to leave the country for an engagement. We learned that Edo de Waart would be returning as guest conductor and would be using his old dressing room in Blomstedt's absence.

Playing on the theme of Maestro Blomstedt being such a religious man, my friends and I made up a large sign saying that Edo's old dressing room had become a meditation center and that Edo could no longer use it to change his clothes. Furthermore, any consumption of adult beverages in the dressing room was prohibited, as was fraternizing with the opposite sex — such as sopranos. It was printed on official management paper. It looked real. We put the sign up in the dressing room to welcome Edo when he arrived.

---

38. Good Stock!

Shortly after Maestro Blomstedt began conducting the San Francisco Symphony Orchestra, my mother came to one of the concerts. After the concert I took her to the dressing room to meet the Maestro. They chatted for a while and Blomstedt looked over at me and said, "I see you come from good stock!"

Speaking of good stock, I've always believed that ancestry can have a lot to do with musical ability or the ability to play an instrument well. As I said in the Prelude, any musical talent I have is a gift from my ancestors.

Recently, Carol and I ran across a letter my mother had written to her piano students in 1963. Reading it, I realized that she had more influence on my musical life than I had ever given her credit for. In fact, it expresses almost word for word in one short paragraph what I've tried to communicate in a whole book. In her letter she told her students this:

> Welcome to my piano class. I hope you will be happy as you learn to play music in your piano study. You take lessons so that you may <u>learn to play with ease in an expressive manner</u>. More than this, your piano study gives you a worthy effort which can enrich and add joy to your life. It strengthens memory, accuracy, precision, and concentration. Through music there is also a spiritual development. One may express one's every mood of joy or sorrow, and one may [g]ain an appreciation of the art of music which is surely a worthy part of all our lives.

Jim Thompson

Years ago at Interlochen, I met a kid from Texas named Jim Thompson. Jim had a few freckles sprinkled over his face and straight blond hair with a cowlick in back that reminded me of Dennis the Menace, in other words an all-American look. I really admired Jim's trumpet playing; he was the best trumpet player there.

Later in my career, I started hearing about a trumpet player named Jim Thompson who had become quite famous, and I wondered if it was the same Jim Thompson I had known as a kid at Interlochen. Then, on a tour with Summit Brass, Jim Thompson was hired as a trumpet player. I could hardly wait to meet him to see if he was the same person I had known at Interlochen.

When I got on the bus, someone pointed him out to me. I knew that Jim had played principal trumpet for the Montreal Symphony and the Atlanta Symphony, and was presently teaching at the Eastman School in Rochester.

I went up to meet him. My God! He didn't look at all like the Jim Thompson I knew from Interlochen. This man was heavy with darker skin and a bit of a belly. He looked like a German butcher. I could picture him behind a meat counter. I told him the story about how I had always wondered if he was the same Jim Thompson I had known at Interlochen. I told him I thought he looked like a German butcher. He said, "I *am!*"

I said, "What do you mean, you are?"

He said, "Because my mother couldn't support me, she gave me to an American airman during the Berlin airlift. He took me home and adopted me. His last name was Thompson, so my name's Jim Thompson." But Jim Thompson was purely German.

He also had a disease of the blood, common mostly to Northern Europeans, where too much hemoglobin builds up. To treat the disease, the patient gives blood every month or two, thus keeping it balanced. Another friend of mine who is German has it too. Jim's doctor told him that he should try to find his biological relatives to get some history on this disease. He hadn't had contact with anyone from his natural family.

Jim told me he thought it strange that he had never had to work hard at playing the trumpet. "I was a natural," he said. "I could play without thinking about it."

While playing with the Atlanta Symphony, they visited Berlin on tour. Somehow he found his mother and made arrangements to meet her for the first time as an adult. She took him back to her apartment where he noticed the walls were decorated with pictures of his relatives, his aunts, uncles, and grandparents. In the photos most of them were holding trumpets.

So tell me ancestry has nothing to do with playing an instrument.

— 39. KURT MASUR AND BACH —

The conductor of the Leipzig Gewandhaus Orchestra, Kurt Masur, often visited the San Francisco Symphony as a guest conductor. This was before his tenure as conductor of the New York Philharmonic. The musicians of the San Francisco Symphony had a good relationship with him. We liked him and he liked us.

Our orchestra went on tour to Germany with Maestro Blomstedt. We were scheduled to play in Leipzig, but Leipzig was in East Germany and we were not allowed to stay there overnight. So we were bused in for the concert.

Kurt had arranged a supper for us in the concert hall for when we arrived in the afternoon. During supper he asked if any of us would like to visit Bach's grave in St. Thomas Church, within walking distance of the Gewandhaus.

Almost everyone in the orchestra wanted to visit, so we all marched down the main street together with Kurt in the lead. Kurt was popular in East Germany because of his efforts toward unification, so people on the street knew him.

While we were walking we encountered the police. Kurt assured them that we were not a demonstration but were his guests.

We entered St. Thomas Church to the strains of Bach. Maestro Masur had arranged for the church organist to play Bach for us when we arrived. What a moving experience! Many of our members were in tears as we stood around Bach's resting place surrounded by Bach's music.

PART VII

ᔕ

MICHAEL TILSON THOMAS
(1996-Present)

40. It's Time!

Finishing up my career with Michael Tilson Thomas was like riding into the sunset to the blazing accompaniment of an emotional Mahler symphony. My last two years in the orchestra were a heady time.

No one was smarter or more talented than Michael, and it's hard to imagine anyone being more emotionally expressive. He would often be in tears during the slow movement of a Mahler symphony. We used to say that he would pee on every tree.

I soon realized that we came from two different cultures of musical expression. Mine was German or horizontal, which is more intellectual and linear, as in Bach Chorales. His was Klezmer (eastern European Jewish) or vertical, which is more soulful and expressive. It was a wonderful two years and we respectfully admired each other.

Michael is gay. The executive director of the orchestra told me that before they hired him, they had to ask him if he had AIDS. AIDS was new then, and the powers that be didn't want to hire somebody who would be wilting at the podium, as they called it. Michael assured them he didn't have AIDS.

I spent my last two years in the orchestra with Michael getting ready to retire. Music, particularly the horn, had been my life, my sustenance, my venue of self-discovery and learning. Through music, doors opened and behind each door was a new situation. I had to figure out who I was and how to survive, from grade school and being dyslexic (better known then as being stupid), to youth, to the pressures of the Fresno Philharmonic, and then suddenly finding myself in the Chicago Symphony Orchestra. Behind each door that opened to me was both a gift and a new challenge where I had to adapt, learn, and create myself anew. But many times I just had to wing it. ...

Playing in the Moment

... like a time late in my career when we were playing a piece by Bernstein that called for a backstage horn solo. I was required to walk offstage, play the solo, and come back onstage.

Well, I knew the solo. I didn't need the music. I'd just walk back and play it. But in rehearsals we had to learn how to get just the right amount of volume from offstage. This meant opening the stage door to the precise width that would create the far-off effect needed for the passage I was playing. The stagehand had to be there to hold the door open.

The first night I went out backstage, and I couldn't find Dennis, the stagehand. I called out to him. He finally came out of his cubbyhole dressed only in his shorts and looking distracted. But he opened the door for me and I played my solo and then went back onstage. Everything was fine.

Afterward I said, "Dennis, what shenanigans do you have planned for me tomorrow night when I do this solo?

He said, "Oh, you just wait and see! I've got something planned for you. It might involve some topless women."

I was leery about what might happen. The time came for the

solo the next night and as I walked off stage, I looked around, and again there was no Dennis. Now what was he up to?

The time came, and I had to begin my solo, but I was concentrating so hard on what Dennis and his friends might do to try to distract me that after a few bars I lost my place and couldn't remember the rest of the tune. I started improvising while trying to get back to where I needed to be in the music. What I was playing wasn't even close to what I was supposed to be playing, but at least it was something.

When I came back onstage everyone in the orchestra was shuffling their feet. This is how orchestra members applaud other orchestra members during a performance. They shuffle their feet. They thought I'd had the nerve to improvise on a Bernstein solo when, in fact, it was all a big mistake. I had lost my place in the music, but I had somehow been able to stay present and play in the moment.

On Retiring before You're Asked

I'd been in the orchestra world long enough to know that there are players in critical positions who refuse to retire despite no longer being able to play up to the standards that made them so famous. They hang on to their jobs and their fame because it seems that they have nothing else in their lives. Their lives have centered around their careers, and the prospect of quitting all of a sudden is very threatening.

If asked the question, "Who are you?" they'll say, for example, "Well, I'm the principal player for the Chicago Symphony Orchestra." The positions they hold become who they are, even outweighing their roles as fathers, mothers, husbands, or wives. Their identity is totally wrapped up in their jobs.

Wanting to escape this fate, I've always felt it was important for me to quit while I was still on top. The last thing I wanted people to say was, "Oh, he should have retired five years ago."

My friend Mark Lawrence and I had an agreement. He sat behind me in the San Francisco Symphony for many years and heard everything I did. He's a good judge of quality. I told him, "Now when you notice that it's not working anymore, you tap me on the shoulder and tell me, 'Dave, it's time.'"

Well, I never got to that point. I began the process of retiring two years before I actually did. That process began with my teaching.

On Teaching

My teaching career began in Chicago at DePaul University while I was with the Chicago Symphony Orchestra. In Detroit I became head of the Brass Department at Wayne State, as well as the horn teacher and brass choir conductor. Our brass choir at Wayne State gave many great concerts, and it was from a poster for one of those concerts that I made the airplane that I sailed past Arthur Fiedler during "The Armed Forces Medley."

When I got to San Francisco I was asked to teach at the San Francisco Conservatory and at San Francisco State. I taught only two years in the mid-1970s at San Francisco State. What affected me most while I was there was that the head of the music department, a very nice man, became extremely ill. His illness was a mystery to the doctors. He had been going from clinic to clinic to find a diagnosis but was only getting progressively worse.

When I visited him, he was wearing a surgical mask, afraid of infecting someone else with whatever he had. Finally, he was diagnosed with one of the first cases of AIDS that anyone knew about, and he died shortly after that. AIDS soon became an epidemic.

I taught at the San Francisco Conservatory for many years and, as head of the brass department, had a wonderful brass choir. Many of my former Conservatory students are still in California, and they play in orchestras up and down the San Joaquin Valley and in the Bay Area. Some of them play in the Fresno Philharmonic.

One day, not long before I retired from teaching at the San Francisco Conservatory, I was rehearsing my brass choir in the auditorium. We were playing a resonant Bach piece with the sound billowing through the room. Suddenly the building started to shake. The lights swayed above our heads. We feared they would drop on us, so we trooped out through the hallway into the parking lot and waited for things to settle down.

That was in October 1989, the day the Loma Prieta earthquake hit the Bay Area. At the time, we had no idea how serious it was or that the San Francisco-Oakland Bay Bridge had collapsed.

The earthquake also interrupted the World Series game between the Giants and the A's. There had been quite a bit of talk the previous week about the brass section from the Symphony possibly being hired to play the Star Spangled Banner at the opening of that game. It didn't happen, but I couldn't help wondering what it would have been like to be stuck in a milling crowd at the stadium in an earthquake.

We cancelled the brass choir rehearsal, and I had to drive home on Nineteenth Avenue toward Marin. Nineteenth Avenue is one stoplight after another, and all of the signals were out, so traffic was snarled. Thankfully I did make it home.

I taught for a long time at the Music Academy of the West in Santa Barbara. Each week we had a masterclass and each student would play. Many of the students were wonderful players and went on to have wonderful jobs. One in particular, Jennifer Montone, became principal horn of the Philadelphia Orchestra.

Somehow in one of my masterclasses I mentioned using a Flowbee, which is a hair cutting machine that hooks up to a vacuum cleaner. I've used it for 35 or 40 years. It sucks the hair up and cuts it off at the desired length.

We ended up giving a student in my masterclass a haircut. The student, Brad Gemeinhardt, is now a member of the horn section in the Metropolitan Opera Orchestra in New York. He recently sent me a birthday greeting asking me if I still gave haircuts.

A couple of years before I retired from the Symphony, I realized that I was starting to lose the detachment I needed in order to teach effectively without picking up too much on the struggles of my students. By being with them, playing along with them, and demonstrating for them, I was beginning to lose my ease of playing.

I realized that if I wanted my final years of playing with the orchestra to be successful, I had to give up teaching. So I began resigning from my teaching positions.

Around the same time, I also realized I had to do something about my drinking. During a season with four concerts a week, I could only drink on the off nights, or three nights a week. When I started dreaming of retiring just so I'd be able to drink on all seven nights of the week, I realized drinking would probably end up killing me. So I decided to join AA. I'd hop on my bike and take the path behind my house to the 7 a.m. meetings. I was in AA for 20 years.

Joining AA was a magical event. I had a great home group up in Marin where I met many wonderful people who became friends. I'd see people come in who were total wrecks, who cowered in a corner not communicating with anyone. Then gradually I'd see a transformation in these people as they quit drinking, and began to open up, communicate, and become leaders of the group.

It was thrilling to watch this happen. Sometimes it would take a year and sometimes just a few weeks.

I've come to believe that hornplaying, especially principal hornplaying, is a young person's job. We can't hang on to these wonderful jobs forever, and there are new players coming up through the ranks who will never have the opportunity if we stay in the job too long.

San Francisco Symphony horn section at my retirement
Left to right: Robert Ward, John Ring, Bruce Roberts, Lori Westin, David Krehbiel

I decided that when I reached the age of 62 and Social Security, I would quit. Forty years is longer than most principal horns last anyway. But no one ever asked me to retire. In fact, Michael Tilson Thomas asked me to stay longer.

Before I left but after I had made the decision to retire, the orchestra's executive director, a high-powered guy named Peter Pastreich, came to me and asked if I could talk to the principal flute player about retiring. Pastreich hadn't had any luck and thought maybe I'd help him out.

The flute player, much older than I, had been asked to retire but refused. In fact, he had hired an attorney to sue for age discrimination.

When Pastreich asked me to try to talk the flute player into retiring, I laughed at him and said, "Are you kidding me? That's not my job; that's your job!" Pastreich made three to five times as much money as I did and now he wanted *me* to ask the flute player to retire? Forget it!

ᕦ

41. Mozart Horn Concerto No. 2

Near the end of my time as principal horn with the San Francisco Symphony Orchestra, I was invited to play a farewell solo at all four of the concerts for one of the last season series. I felt honored. I chose the Mozart Horn Concerto No. 2, and Michael Tilson Thomas conducted. Before the first of the concerts, 40 or 50 horn

FORTY
HORN PLAYERS
FROM
ALL OVER
CALIFORNIA
PAY TRIBUTE TO
RETIRING
SF SYMPHONY
PRINCIPAL HORN
DAVE KREHBIEL

players from the area showed up in front of the concert hall to serenade me in honor of my retirement and 40 years playing, 25 of which were in San Francisco.

Of the many solo performances I'd done with the SFO, I think this was the most musical I'd ever played. I'd performed the Mozart 2nd Concerto many times over the years, and each performance was different because of changes I'd made at the last moment while performing. This always gave me the feeling that I was composing while I was playing. But the performances at my farewell concerts were in a league of their own musically and represented the culmination of a lifetime's devotion to embracing the concepts of ease of playing and Creative Not Caring.

At Home on the Kings River — 1998

I retired in 1998 after 25 years as principal horn with the San Francisco Symphony Orchestra. Carol and I moved back to our home town of Reedley, to be with our many friends and relatives, and to live on our 18 acres on the Kings River. My brother-in-law, who is a contractor, built a garage with an apartment above, which was ready for us in the summer of 1998.

We lived in that apartment for three years while we designed and built our dream house overlooking the River. I also had a "bucket list" of activities lined up for retirement in addition to

David and Carol Krehbiel

building our river house. I could never understand why people stopped working when they retired.

Flying was high on my list, so I took flying lessons. An old friend of mine from high school now owned two planes. He and I built a Kolb Ultralight which I flew for a while. But I'm sorry to say I never got a license. I finished everything but the test.

Maybe flying was a little too much like playing the horn under stressful conditions, and maybe the consequences of Creative Not Caring failing me at a crucial moment when I was flying an airplane were a lot more serious than a rough slur or clam.

I found that flying and riding motorcycles were similar in that there came a time when I figured I wasn't safe to do either one of them anymore.

Ready to fly my Ultralight!

42. PLAY BALL!

Part of my retirement agreement with the Symphony was that for the next four years, if they needed a player to fill in for a week or two, they would ask me first. If I accepted the engagement, they would pay me at my old salary rate, which was good. But since I lived 200 miles away now, I wasn't tempted to hang around the orchestra much. I did like coming in and playing two or three weeks of concerts every year just to see how things were going and to visit with old friends.

For the opening concert of the season in September 2001, the San Francisco Symphony Orchestra had programmed Mahler's Sixth Symphony. This piece required a couple of extra horns, so I was invited to play. I accepted, which meant I would have to get up at 5:00 a.m. and drive from Reedley to San Francisco, arriving in time for 10:00 rehearsals on Saturday, Tuesday, and Wednesday.

On Tuesday, September 11th, I had been driving for a couple of hours or so when I stopped for my usual cup of coffee at a service station in Los Banos. The TV at the station was playing. Usually I ignored it, got my coffee and left. But that morning something on the screen caught my attention. I was shocked to see the two jets diving into the Twin Towers in New York. I knew this event signaled a national upheaval of some sort, but I couldn't stay to watch. I had to get in the car and keep going if I wanted to arrive at rehearsal on time. As far as I could tell, this incident had happened on the East Coast and wouldn't affect my ability to make it into San Francisco.

After I drove for another hour or so, my wife Carol called to tell me that the Symphony had notified her that rehearsal was cancelled. The bridges into San Francisco were closed, and the city was shut down. So I turned around and went home. By Friday of that week, the orchestra had decided to go ahead and take the chance of having a rehearsal that morning and a concert that evening. So I got up early on Friday again and headed back to San Francisco for that morning's rehearsal.

We all knew Mahler's Sixth but hadn't played it in a couple of years. We would be under-rehearsed, having had only two rehearsals for the concerts that week instead of the usual four, but I knew the performances would be spectacular because of the emotional tension stirred up by the events of the last few days. Stressful circumstances like this can bring out an orchestra's ability to play magically, like a massive chamber ensemble, and I knew all the musicians would have their antennae deployed.

The audience was on edge, too. It took a lot of courage for them to cross the bridges that night, drive through the snarled traffic, and pile into a crowded concert hall. Was someone lurking nearby waiting to blow up something else?

It was the custom of the San Francisco Symphony to open the first concert of the season with "The Star-Spangled Banner," but this time, Michael Tilson Thomas made a change. Instead of playing the "banner" at the usual full volume, muted strings played it in a reverent *sotto voce* (very quietly). The effect was so incredible and so emotional that the audience and orchestra members alike were tearing up. It set the perfect atmosphere to begin a concert in these troubled circumstances.

As the last notes of "The Star-Spangled Banner" died away and everyone was sitting in quiet contemplation, a resounding voice from the top of the hall suddenly called out "Play ball!" It was like hearing a giant balloon pop. The mood was shattered. The orchestra's ability to work magic in the concert that night was ruined. We could only go through the motions.

Michael and the orchestra members were really upset. How could this happen? After the concert, we gathered backstage and lamented that one person had been able to ruin our expectations of performing a concert people would never forget. What kind of idiot would do that?

I played the next week's concerts with the Symphony, too, rising early to drive to the rehearsal on Tuesday. As I walked in, I joined some other orchestra members who were reading a note on the bulletin board.

The note was from a woman who had attended the concert

with her father. She apologized for his outburst, claiming he had Alzheimer's disease and thought he was at a baseball game. What could we say? We read the note, turned, and walked away.

When you perform in a group at the level of the San Francisco Symphony, you begin to take for granted a certain level of excellence and musicality. An incident like this makes you realize and appreciate how delicate and fragile great performances really are.

——— 43. COLBURN SCHOOL ———

After I had been retired from the San Francisco Symphony for a few years and wasn't playing any more, I was invited to teach at Colburn, a music conservatory in downtown Los Angeles adjacent to the Museum of Contemporary Art and across the street from the Walt Disney Concert Hall.

The conservatory is named for a businessman named Richard D. Colburn, who made his money in the insurance world. He was a successful businessman with a passion for classical music. He assisted in the creation of this conservatory, where all student expenses, including room and board, were paid for. The school auditioned students from all over the world, and had the top musicians.

I would drive down from Reedley to Bakersfield, take the Amtrak bus over the Grapevine to Union Station, and then hop onto a little bus over to Colburn. My office was on the third floor facing north and had a wonderful view of the Walt Disney Concert Hall. I'm sure the students were inspired to have this beautiful hall designed by architect Frank Gehry and home of the Los Angeles Philharmonic across the street from their school.

Teaching there was a challenging new experience for me because I had to learn to teach without demonstrating since I didn't play anymore. I could only teach by talking and singing. Many of my students from Colburn are now playing in major orchestras.

I had come to feel that for me to teach in conservatories was unethical because my students didn't have much of an opportunity to make a living at what they were studying, much less the ability to pay off their education. I could have rationalized and said, "Well, I'm teaching them more than how to play the horn. I'm teaching them about how to handle their lives," but I wasn't okay with students saddling themselves with enormous debt to earn a degree in music and then being unable to use what I was teaching them to pay off the debt.

However, at Colburn things were different. Everything at Colburn, including room and board, was paid for. These excellent students were obtaining their training debt-free. They were there to succeed, to do the best they could, and it didn't have to be on their conscience — or mine — that they were incurring debt.

After a while it became quite difficult for me to commute to Los Angeles every week. I decided that when the opportunity came I would retire from teaching at Colburn, but that I would not do so until I found the right person to replace me.

The Los Angeles Philharmonic hired a new principal horn player, Andrew Bain. I heard him play and I knew he was the one who could replace me. He also had the advantage of working with the Philharmonic right across the street and could have these talented students come in and play "extra" with the orchestra to learn what it was like to play at a professional level.

We held a teaching audition for Mr. Bain with some of the faculty and myself on stage. He taught a lesson while we watched and listened. The student would play something and he would make recommendations. What sold me was that one student played a horn excerpt from Puccini's *Tosca* and played it quite well, but Andrew said, "Well, how about if you played it like this?" And then he played it. It was phenomenal. Every note had a purpose. It was so subtle and so musical that I was sold right away. What I really didn't want was for new faculty to come in merely teaching notes and how to blow the horn. I wanted someone who would teach music, and that is what he did. So I happily retired from teaching at Colburn.

After I finished at Colburn, they asked me to come back for graduation ceremonies. I didn't have any students graduating at that time and I didn't want to drive all the way down to LA for a graduation. I was retired and didn't have much to do with the school anymore. But they begged. *Please come to the graduation.* So I went.

At the ceremony, they put a robe on me, handed me a scepter, and told me to lead the faculty through the auditorium and onto the stage. I'd been sitting on the stage, holding on to my scepter and not paying much attention to what was being said in the ceremony, when it finally sunk in that I was the person they were talking about from the podium. I was being awarded an Honorary Doctorate degree.

This was evidently the first Honorary Doctorate degree Colburn had bestowed. And it was a real degree, the Dean assured my wife when she asked. After a few speeches, they put a doctoral cape over my shoulders.

It was an honor, but it felt sort of like a practical joke, too. Everybody was in on the secret. Even my wife knew ahead of time. But no one had told me.

My family at our 50th wedding anniversary.
Left to right: Lee, Kristin, David, Carol, Art

POSTLUDE

The United States waged a war of retaliation for the 3,000 deaths and the havoc wreaked by the events of 9/11. Some of our family's friends from Reedley formed a group protesting that war. When we moved back to Reedley, we joined the group, which became known as the Reedley Peace Center.

I still didn't have much tolerance for fundamentalist religions — after all, that was part of why I'd left Reedley — but I found that something new had sprung up there while I was gone. Most of the Peace Center members also attended a Sunday school class at my old church. They encouraged me to check it out, and I found that the people in this class were looking for answers to the same questions I'd lived with all my life. The only difference was that they were looking for those answers in the context of the religion I had renounced many years before. It seemed that this group and I had been leading parallel wanderings.

In college I had decided that religion, especially Christianity, wasn't for me because of the conflict it had engendered in mankind over the years. When I got to Chicago, I had no time or psychic energy for contemplating the meaning of life. I was much too preoccupied with learning how to play the horn in a way that would allow me to survive in my career.

In Detroit, when I was able to relax a little with my music, Carol and I gradually began to consider that maybe we could be involved in something outside ourselves that contributed to mankind. We found that the Unitarian Church filled that need. There, we became involved with human rights concerns and race relations, specifically the grape boycott of that time. We were torn about the grape boycott issue because my wife's father, Roy Smeds, was a farmer producing grapes in California.

At that same time, Roy was becoming involved with the farm workers' union in California. He was the first grower in the Reedley area to drive the 100 mile round trip south to Delano, walk into Cesar Chavez's office, and ask to sign a contract with the farm workers for his farm. He was a radical in that he believed if he paid more to his workers, the time that he spent on a tractor working his fields would be worth more. But this went against the leanings of most of the farming industry in the central San Joaquin Valley. Because Roy's grapes were now union grapes, he was ostracized by peers, neighbors, and friends.

Since things were getting to be a little easier with my profession and our kids getting a little older, I started having more time to contemplate the *whys*. Why are we here? Why are we on the planet?

When we moved to San Francisco, I became fascinated with the books of Carlos Casteneda. Also, I was introduced to the work of George Gurdjieff, and Carol and I began to participate in Gurdjieff's meetings, meditation, and sacred dancing. Then through a friend I became interested in the occult and with the help of a ouija board made contact through a medium with an entity named Michael, a benevolent being who answered any questions I would ask about my past lives, my last performance, different horns, or the different mouthpieces I was using on them. I could ask him about any individual including my children and he would give a readout of their progressions through their many lives.

Carol and I were part of a group in the Bay Area interested in the occult that met every other week. When we left there at retirement, we left the group too. We still go back every once in a while, but we are not part of the main group any more. Other interests have taken its place.

As I studied other disciplines and religions, I found many of the answers my religious upbringing had been unable to provide. Through reading the work of Eckhart Tolle in *The Power of Now* and *Practicing the Power of Now,* I am realizing the oneness of all religions and that people of all religions, including Christianity, have been saying the same things but in different ways.

Because of this, I find that for the first time in my life I am comfortable attending a church service, though I wouldn't call myself an evangelical or a true believer. In the Sunday school class, I was able to find an esoteric meaning to the teachings of Jesus that for the first time made sense of Christianity for me. This Sunday school class and the church to which I returned now promote acceptance of all religions, all races, and all sexual orientations. This is more than tolerance. I would call it more like the understanding that we are all one.

Still, rather than finding me in a Sunday school class looking for answers, you'll probably find me sitting and meditating in the basement prayer room. Sometimes people join me. Sometimes they don't.

What I love most about church is still the music. When I came back to Reedley, I found myself singing in the church choir again, which presented a problem for me since most of my musical life had been pitched in the key of F. I could no longer look at a note and hear the pitch in my head, and if I did, it was a 4th off. I found myself trying to transpose as I sang, but with my dyslexia problem (which I finally understood after many years of agony), transposing to find the right pitch while reading the words at the same time was a challenge.

The one thing I did have was a sense of intonation, and I would become quite frustrated when choir members would start to sing flat and the pitch of the group would begin to sink. I must add that sometimes I forget that I am 83 years old now and often I'm the oldest one in any group, when for so long I was the "kid" in the orchestra.

Now that I've retired, I've come into an even greater love of music, and listening to music has become more enjoyable, intense, and even spiritual. This joy of listening comes from hearing the humanness in the music and feeling the emotion of the composer and performer.

Listening has become an esoteric experience, and the slightest unexpected nuance can take my breath away. I worked all my career to strengthen the humanness and emotional expression in my playing. Now when I listen, I hear new depths in a piece of music that I'd never heard before.

I found that to get at the humanness in a piece of music, I had to learn to play with what I called Creative Not Caring, or getting past my ego's need to deliver a perfect performance. My goal became communicating with the audience from my soul and the soul of the composer. Communicating what was true in each moment became more important than how things turn out in the end.

Just because I have told these stories from my past doesn't mean that I live there. Performing music gave me the opportunity to observe the voice in my head that tried to take me out of the present and focus on the future or the past. I still wish to live in the present, maintaining the attitude of Creative Not Caring. Yet it has been fun to reminisce about how I got to this particular here and now. I have been fortunate indeed to be living this life.

A few years ago, the Westminster College Choir came to the refurbished auditorium at the former Fresno State campus in Fresno, California. I believe it was the most incredible choir concert I have ever heard, from the staging to the repertoire to the performance. I was in heaven. I just couldn't believe any performance could be so wonderful.

During the concert, the conductor, Joe Miller, said that he felt he had roots in California because his first job was as choral conductor at Stanislaus State, which is in Turlock, a small town in the middle of California's San Joaquin Valley. My question was, "How did this guy get from being a sort of junior professor in Turlock to the top of his profession, conducting Westminster Choir and performing regular concerts with the New York Philharmonic?" He was at the top. How did this happen to him?

I waited until after the concert, and when I found him I asked, "How did you get from Stanislaus to Westminster?" He told me, "The doors just opened and I walked through them." And I thought, *My God! Yes! That's just what happened to me!* The doors to these opportunities just opened. I always knew there would be a lesson I had to learn about myself on the other side in order to succeed, but I walked through to meet whatever awaited me there.

It is my sincere hope that the doors will remain open to each of you who open yourselves to all possibilities in the universe.

"You are not IN the universe, you ARE the universe — an intrinsic part of it. Ultimately you are not a person, but a focal point where the universe is becoming conscious of itself. What an amazing miracle."

—*Eckhart Tolle.*

Life on the Farm.

APPENDIX A

Terms

Creative Not Caring

- Staying in the present moment.

- Not minding what happens after this moment or what happened before.

- Trusting your body to play the instrument.

- Using your thinking to power musical emotion.

- Using your thinking for time and space in the ensemble.

Playing in the Moment

- Not playing safe. Going for the music.

- Taking chances while playing, as when I slurred using a new technique while performing Beethoven 2. You are also composing at this moment.

- Occupying your mind with the emotion the composer is communicating in the passage. This, in turn, keeps thoughts of what might happen before and after the audition or performance at bay. When I am in the present, playing how I feel musically right now, it's one of the most conscious, most alive times I can have.

Ease of Playing

- A balance between three variables: motivation, vibration, and resonance.

- Using air, vibration, and resonance, each to their maximum efficiency.

- Realizing that if one of these factors (air, vibration, resonance) are not at their maximum efficiency, the other two must work much harder to compensate.

- Conquering fear. Never mind what happened before or what will happen next.

- Trusting the body to take over physically and play. This is analogous to learning how to ride a bicycle; once you learn, your body knows how. If you try to think about keeping your balance on a bicycle, you will be too slow and you will fall.

- Experimenting and taking a chance on making a change to become more efficient. (Creative Not Caring.)

- Not practicing old habits and reinforcing them.

Playing Musically

- Balancing the vertical with the horizontal.

- Being able to feel the flavor of each note while remaining conscious of the line or phrase.

- Being able to feel the gravitational pull from one note to the other, going and coming.

- Creating tension and releasing tension in a musical phrase like breathing in and out.

- Using tone color, volume, and inflection as an actor would do to portray emotion.

- Becoming involved with the emotion of the music, which is the best way to alleviate stage fright.

- Being aware of feeling or feeling the architecture of each phrase and composition.

The Voice in Your Head

- Be able to recognize that the voice in your head is the cause of most trouble with nerves and stage fright.

- Be aware that the voice in your head is not who you are.

APPENDIX B

A Horn Player's Helpful Hints

- To improve sound, relax face muscles.

- To relax facial tension, open eyes very wide and hold open.

- For body resonance, drop shoulders and relax the body.

- To balance body tension, push out gently in the naval area.

- To release upper body tension, have someone push down hard on your shoulders while playing.

- To relieve tension, inhale through nose seven counts; hold four counts; exhale eight counts.

- When starting a note by yourself, think of your rectal area.

- For efficiency, think about the airstream rubbing across your lips.

- For efficiency, make a raspy buzz on the mouthpiece like a bassoon reed.

- Do a valve trill, then lip trill connecting air on lip trill.

- Gliss harmonic series up to 16th partial, connecting slurs and high register.

Consciousness

- For connecting to the music, observe your emotion at this moment.
- For discovering your motivation, observe what you are thinking about at this moment.

Play by Memory

- Get your head away from the notes.
- Become aware of your body.
- Feel the emotion in the music.
- Not looking at the notes on the page gives freedom to feel emotion.
- Things don't seem as difficult when you aren't looking at the notes.
- Never play when your embouchure is tired. When your legs are sore from running, you don't cure them by running harder.
- Seek progress by detachment. You can't improve the experience of riding a bicycle by having to think of balance.
- If you are getting tired, the motivation, vibration, and resonance are not ideal in relation to each other.
- Ease of playing is not getting tired.
- Ease of playing is being in balance with motivation, vibration, and resonance, each ideal for range and volume.

- Getting tired is having one or more of the variables — motivation, vibration, and resonance — not doing its job properly.

- Whistle the harmonic series and feel the airstream with your hand.

- Deliberately miss a note and see how difficult it is to do.

- Your ego won't let you miss notes. Take a chance and ignore the ego.

- Play a note and feel it get pregnant and give birth to the next note.

- Go from one note to the next like inhaling then exhaling.

APPENDIX C

Motivation, Vibration, Resonance

Producing a pitched sound on an instrument requires three variables: motivation, vibration, and resonance. Unlike a stringed instrument, where manipulation of these variables is visible, most of what we as horn players do while playing is happening internally or hidden behind the mouthpiece. I like to use string playing as an easy way to visualize the analogous process of hornplaying.

Motivation

In motivation, the motion of the bow as it is drawn across the strings serves the same function as air moving across the embouchure for horn players.

Much has been written about breathing and the use of air in brass playing. In my experience, it is again a question of balancing the body tension required for breath support and the relaxation necessary for free and resonant sound production. If the air is brought up to the embouchure under too much pressure, this pressure must be controlled by resistance which in turn creates tension.

To help find the balance between relaxation and supporting the breath, I think of the body as a U-shaped magnet where all the positive, relaxed energy is at the point of vibration, and the negative, tensed energy is focused on the muscle group that we use for support. Imagine the air stream at the lips as the positive pole, the diaphragm as the negative pole, and the space between the two poles — the shoulders, throat, torso, etc. — is relaxed and inert.

I achieve this feeling of balance by pushing out gently on the front of the belly and dropping the shoulders. Try it and see if it works for you.

Vibration

In vibration, the violin string is like the embouchure (the thing that does the vibration). The bow catches the strings, pulling and stretching, until they snap back, causing the vibration. The embouchure does the same when it is stretched by the airstream, a puff of air is released causing a vibration.

With the string, as with the embouchure, tension and thickness affect the vibration rate.

One exercise I suggest is opening your eyes as wide as you can while playing, just to make yourself aware both mentally and physically of the unwanted tension you might be using.

The release of that excess, unnecessary tension can dramatically open up your sound.

Resonance

Resonance is like the string length, which is like the resonating volume inside the mouth and inside the body. String length is analogous to the resonant volume inside the mouth. The pitch of a given string is changed by changing its length on the fingerboard. We don't change the pitch of a given string by changing its tension. We would need to tighten the string four times as tight to raise the vibration level an octave or double this vibration. The string needs to be the ideal length thickness, and tension for the pitch.

String length is analogous to the diameter of the mouthpiece in brass playing. Just as the pitch results from the thickness and tension of the string, in brass playing the pitch is the function of the embouchure.

So how do we as brass players change our resonant length? The resonant length change must take place behind the mouthpiece. Whistling different pitches is essentially changing the resonant length. You might say that the length of the tube changes the pitch, which is somewhat true. However, we as horn players are able to play up to 16 different pitches of the harmonic series on one length of tube. Lip tension does not change the pitch of the whistle.

The best sound and the greatest ease of playing comes from an ideal motivation (air), and ideal embouchure (string), and the resonant volume inside the mouth and body.

The perfect balance of these three factors for the pitch and volume I call ease of playing.

Helpful Hints: Think of the violin bow when changing oral resonance. Imagine the bow placement, pressure and speed to be like airstream. When visualizing how the airstream rubbing across the embouchure creates a vibration, try thinking of the many variables of the way a bow catches a string.

First, there is the placement of the bow for maximum efficiency, not too close to the bridge and not too far from the center. Then there is bow speed and bow pressure along with the amount of hair on the string. And again, all these factors are variable, depending upon string thickness, tension, volume, and register.

Keeping a motivating air stream focused on the embouchure while changing resonance inside the mouth is a bit like rubbing your stomach and patting your head at the same time. Aiming and focusing the air stream is essential for maximum efficiency.

We have all had the experience of trying to play a high note and nothing comes out. If there is too much pressure and too much embouchure tension, there is no vibration.

We give away most of our efficiency going from one partial to the next one above. Learning to do glisses through the partial series without stopping the air and creating excess tension is the key.

Of the three variables, the resonant volume in the chamber of the mouth requires the least physical effort. It is my go-to principal for ease of playing.

In general, we talk about changing resonance in the mouth by "dropping the jaw" in the low register or using a shallow vowel sound in the high register, such as "e" instead of "o."

Whistling is a more intuitive and specific way of understanding how we change the volume in the mouth to produce different pitches. When we whistle, our whistling "embouchure" remains quite still as we whistle through the different registers.

The tongue and jaw are most active and responsible for manipulating volume in the mouth. As the pitch goes higher, the tongue rises in the mouth, directing the air through a narrower channel near the soft palate and then forward in the mouth behind the aperture. In the high register, it's ideal to feel the air moving forward and into "the mask" or the sinus cavity with the same sensation we have when singing in a loud falsetto voice.

Like a perfectly smooth glissando on a stringed instrument, it is a great exercise to create that uninterrupted siren-like sound and flow of air while whistling, buzzing the lips independently or through the mouthpiece. Once we put all this wonderful, natural vibration into the brass amplifier that is our instrument, we have even more fun blowing up and down through the harmonic series. We can feel the "pop" of notes as they lock in at the moment our gliss hits their organic frequencies.

Another way to think about resonance as a means to efficiency is to consider the principle of sympathetic vibration. We have all experienced this at some point, intentionally or not, by having the snare drum rattle on certain notes or, for example, playing a piano with the dampers off. One can set specific strings in a piano to motion by producing a sound of the same frequency in proximity to the strings. The standing string will respond sympathetically to the motion of your sound wave as the vibrations push against it at the same beats per second.

Instead of strings, the horn has a set of standing nodes at different points in the horn where the sound waves break into the next partial of the harmonic series for that length of tubing. We can force these sound waves to break by intensifying the pressure or volume of the air through the aperture as we play, putting the payload almost entirely on the embouchure, or, we can set up the sympathetic resonance in our mouth and move up and down between the nodal points with less pressure on the embouchure, less strain on soft tissue vibrating inside the mouthpiece and a freer, more open, and more natural sound.

Each note "tastes" different from the next and has a different feel inside the mouth. If we isolate this variable in our playing by exhaling (no air), moving the mouthpiece to the side of our mouth where the aperture has no support (no embouchure) and discover that we can still get around the horn quite flexibly with an untrained, air-starved lip, albeit with no sound quality, projection, or accuracy.

The point is, we can initiate the desired frequency in the horn by producing the same frequency in our mouth, in the same way we can produce a tight, muscle-bound note by using just the embouchure (no resonance or projection), or by forcing the air through the aperture which we must hold in place by pressing on the mouthpiece (no dynamics, no nuance, accuracy, or endurance).

Therefore, ease of playing is only possible when the three principals — air, lips, and resonance — are ideally balanced for the pitch and volume desired. If just one of these variables is not optimal, the other two have to work harder to compensate, and effort comes into our playing.

Ease isn't easy. We have to let go of our tendency to exert ourselves at these moments and find the easy way, trust that it is there, and not give into the idea of working harder. It takes awareness to play with ease, curiosity, and patience to find this balance and focused practice to stay in it once we find it.

— APPENDIX D —

Harmonic Series/Just Intonation

Wind instruments like the horn make a sound when the column of air inside them is excited into resonating or vibrating in a standing wave. The wave vibrates at a certain frequency determined by the length of the instrument's tubing. For brass instruments, "buzzing" the lips at one end of the tube provides the vibration that excites the wave into resonating.

The lowest note that a given length of tubing can produce, called the fundamental, sounds when the player's lips vibrate at the right frequency to excite the air column in the tube into resonating along its entire length.

However, by buzzing the lips at a higher frequency, a player can force the tube to resonate at divisions of its overall length, thus producing higher notes. These divisions are called overtones or partials. The partials represent the numerical fraction of the overall length that the player has excited into vibration according to whether the tube is now vibrating in a wave along one half of its length, or one third of its length, or one quarter, and so on.

We horn players are sometimes called upon to make our instrument vibrate at frequencies as high as one sixteenth of the overall length! The sequence of these fractions or partials, and the particular notes they produce, are what is called the natural harmonic series (see images below).

The harmonies that help make music so pleasing to the ear

sound the purest when the individual notes that are played together to make a chord are tuned so as to match this natural harmonic series. This is what we refer to as *just* intonation. When tuned purely according to just intonation, the notes of a chord resonate together to generate what are called resultant and difference tones that open up a whole new spectrum of sonic delight.

Unfortunately for lovers of harmonic purity, however, modern musical instruments are not tuned to conform to this natural series. In order to allow instruments to play equally well in any of the twelve possible keys of the chromatic scale, they are tuned according to a system called equal temperament, which compromises the purity of the harmonies that result when the notes are sounded together in a chord. A chord in which the notes are tuned according to equal temperament doesn't resonate as pleasingly as it does when tuned according to the natural harmonic series, or just intonation.

Since much brass music tends to be harmonic in nature, we brass players tend to prioritize the harmony in how we tune a particular note we're playing. When we play a chord together, we like to adjust our individual notes to conform to just intonation so we can get the lovely resonance that results.

In contrast, players of other instrument groups tend to hear the music more melodically, which results in their ears being more attuned to equal temperament. That's why we brass players are often at loggerheads with conductors such as Fieldler or de Waart, who didn't start their careers as brass players and tend to be less sensitive to whether chords are tuned according to just intonation.

The contention often centers around the interval of the third in a major chord because this interval is the one most noticeably corrupted by the equal temperament tuning system. An equal-tempered major third is fourteen percent sharper than a just major third, and as we have seen, that fourteen percent can be the cause of much dissent!

The History of Music and the Harmonic Series

Now I would like to propose a rough correlation between the progression of the harmonic series and the history of music, from single melody to advanced harmony and 12-tone music.

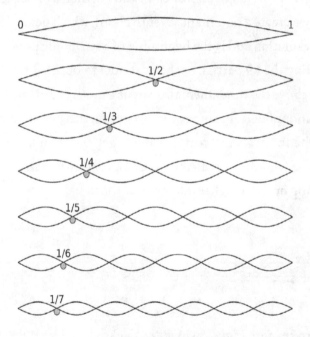

For many centuries, music was represented by chant, a single melody with no harmony, corresponding to the fundamental of the natural harmonic series. Later, the single-note chant evolved to be sung in octaves, which is analogous to the fundamental and second partial. For the sake of clarity, let's refer to the partials numerically, so that in this case #1 would be the fundamental and #2 would be the 2nd partial (see the next image). Let me add here that the minute presence and resonance of these overtones in any given pitch determines the tone quality of the sound.

The #3 partial sounds the interval of a perfect fifth above the #2 partial and a perfect fourth below the #4 partial. This corresponds to the later development in music of chanting in parallel fourths and fifths. Moving up to the #5 partial, which is a major third above the #4, gives us a major chord, C, E, and G. Then by adding the #7 partial, we create a dominant seventh chord, which demands a harmonic resolution and is the beginning of a harmonic progression.

Adding the #9 partial, or the next note to occur above C three octaves above the fundamental, gives us a ninth chord and the start of jazz and modern harmony. As we get further up the harmonic series, the intervals between the notes get closer and closer. This evokes the whole tone scale, then the 12-tone chromatic scale, and then going up even higher into quarter tones.

Courtesy MusicMaker5376 at the English language Wikipedia.

The shape of the horn is a bit like the shape of this historical progression in that for a long portion, the tubing is cylindrical or melody only. Then it gradually begins to become more conical, adding the intervals of the third, fourth, and fifth. Finally it flares quickly out into the bell shape, which gets us past the 16th partial into half-steps and quarter steps.

So the shape of the horn and the harmonic series represent the shape of the chronology of music history from melody only to the explosion of the melodic and harmonic possibilities in the 20th and 21st centuries as represented by the bell flare.

INDEX